Discourse and Its Presuppositions

Discourse and Its Presuppositions

by Charles Landesman

New Haven and London, Yale University Press

1972

To my mother and father

Contents

Preface

This book is an attempt to develop a framework for understanding the nature of meaning and symbolism. The basic argument of Part I yields the conclusion that human action and its psychological conditions are basic constituents of that framework. Part II discusses several fundamental objections to this conclusion and develops some of its implications. In order to keep the main philosophical issues in view, I have abstained from providing a complete survey of the recent literature on the topic and have cited only those writings that were useful in developing the argument.

Several pages of this volume have been adapted from articles I have published, namely, "The Problem of Universals," in *The Problem of Universals,* edited by Charles Landesman (New York: Basic Books, 1971); "Abstract Particulars," *Philosophy and Phenomenological Research,* forthcoming; "Scepticism about Meaning: Quine's Thesis of Indeterminacy," *Australasian Journal of Philosophy* 48 (December 1970): 320-37.

The work on this book was partially supported by a grant in the City University of New York Faculty Research Award Program.

Part I

The Principles of Discourse

1 Propositions

Psychologism and Meaning

Consider the sentence "The shooting of the hunters was quite distressing." For someone unaware of the context in which it was uttered this sentence could be ambiguous; the listener could take it to mean either that the hunters were shot and this was distressing or that the hunters were shooting and this was distressing. It seems that the only way the listener could dispel the ambiguity would be to discover the intention with which the speaker uttered the sentence; by discovering the speaker's intention he would learn which of the two statements was actually made. Since the same sentence is being used to make two different statements, it seems that the difference between the statements themselves is actually constituted by the different intentions with which the sentence is uttered.

In recent philosophy of language there has been a marked tendency to reject theories of language that attempt to explain such phenomena as meaning and ambiguity in terms of the mental states of speakers. Thus our apparently commonsensical account of the ambiguity of "The shooting of the hunters was quite distressing" would be suspect because it makes essential use of the concept of *intention.* Theories and explanations of this type are often castigated as examples of *psychologism,* or *mentalism,* labels applied to those views that fail to concede the independence of logical phenomena, such as meaning, from psychological phenomena, such as thinking, feeling, and willing.

A well-known example of psychologism is provided by the following passages from Hobbes:

1

The general use of speech, is to transfer our mental discourse, into verbal; or the train of our thoughts, into a train of words.

A name is a word taken at pleasure to serve for a mark, which may raise in our mind a thought like to some thought we had before, and which being pronounced to others, may be to them a sign of what thought the speaker had or had not before in his mind.

When a man, upon hearing of any speech, hath those thoughts which the words of that speech and their connections were ordained and constituted to signify, then he is said to understand it; *understanding* being nothing else but conception caused by speech.[1]

For Hobbes, the function of speech is to express our thoughts; words are the signs of thoughts; communication consists in one person informing another of his thoughts. Hobbes's reason for adopting a psychologistic approach is merely hinted at in this passage:

But seeing names ordered in speech . . . are signs of our conceptions, it is manifest they are not signs of the things themselves; for that the sound of this word *stone,* should be the sign of a stone, cannot be understood in any sense but this, that he that hears it collects that he that pronounces it thinks of a stone.[2]

Although the argument implicit in the passage is not at all clear, there is a philosophically interesting reconstruction of it that goes like this: words have meaning only by convention; that the word "stone" can be used to signify a stone is not

1. Thomas Hobbes, *Selections,* ed. F. J. E. Woodbridge (New York: Scribner, 1930), pp. 165, 15, 173.
    2. Ibid., p. 16.

based upon any of its intrinsic features but upon the conventions people follow when using the word. But, we might well ask, how can conventions bring it about that "stone" means stone? One answer is that when a person is merely thinking of a stone, or when he has formed a mental image of a stone, the relation of the thought or image to what it is about is natural, not to be explained in terms of conventions. The word "stone" can come to signify a stone provided that the word acquires a conventional association with a thought or an image that has meaning independently of conventions. The strength of psychologism is that it can provide an explanation of the phenomenon of conventional meaning; and the reason it is able to do so is that it rests its explanation on something whose meaning or "aboutness" or intentionality does not have to be explained by reference to conventions.[3] Of course, this reconstruction of Hobbes's argument leaves important questions unanswered: How do words come to acquire their conventional associations with thoughts, and in what do these associations consist? How do thoughts come to have a natural meaning? What does natural meaning consist in? These questions will arise again later.

3. Bertrand Russell accepts a distinction between conventional and natural meaning: "In the case of words, the relation to what is meant is in the nature of a social convention, and is learned by hearing speech, whereas in the case of ideas the relation is "natural"; i.e. it does not depend upon the behavior of other people, but upon intrinsic similarity and (one might suppose) upon physiological processes existing in all human beings, and to a lesser extent in the higher animals." *Human Knowledge: Its Scope and Limits* (New York: Simon and Schuster, 1962), p. 96. Russell's explanation of natural meaning is of doubtful value. First, it is not clear in what sense the idea of a stone can be similar to a stone. And second, even if the two are similar, this would no more show that the idea signifies the stone than the stone the idea.

Why have so many contemporary philosophers rejected
psychologism? One reason is the popularity of a behavior-
ist approach to psychological analysis, in which explanations
of human actions are couched in terms of behavioral propensities rather than in terms of mental states such as intentions or ideas. Some versions of behaviorism, however,
do not exactly deny the existence of mental states but
rather construe them as being identical with the very behavioral propensities cited in explanations—for example, a
belief is analyzed as a propensity to say or to do certain
things. Whatever their defects, these versions are at least
compatible with psychologism; the incompatible versions
are the tough-minded varieties that fail to acknowledge the
reality of states of mind.

A second reason that psychologism is often rejected is
founded upon the quest for objectivity in the theory of
meaning. In some sense the meanings of words and sentences
are *objective*; that is, they can be common to different persons. Normally, one person does not have to investigate
what is in the mind of another in order for him to grasp
what the other means. Moreover, speakers of a language
usually select words and form sentences in terms of their
antecedently given meanings; these meanings, then, could
not very well be located in their minds. Meanings are selected by speakers, discovered by auditors, and in neither
case are they created by any mental act.

Gottlob Frege put this well when he wrote:

> Psychological logic is on the wrong track entirely if
> it conceives subject and predicate of a judgment as
> ideas in the psychological sense, . . . psychological con-
> siderations have no more place in logic than they do in
> astronomy or geology. If we want to emerge from the
> subjective at all, we must conceive of knowledge as an

activity that does not create what is known but grasps
what is already there. . . . That which we grasp with the
mind also exists independently of this activity, independently of the ideas and their alterations that are a
part of this grasping or accompany it.[4]

A third reason, also stated by Frege and later echoed by
Rudolf Carnap and Ludwig Wittgenstein, is that since a word
is associated with different ideas and images for different
speakers, depending upon their backgrounds and interests,
its meaning cannot be identified with any one of these.

A painter, a horseman, and a zoologist will probably con-
nect different ideas with the name "Bucephalus." This
constitutes an essential distinction between the idea and
the sign's sense, which may be the common property of
many and therefore is not part of a mode of the individual mind.[5]

Objective Meanings

Earlier, the ambiguity of "The shooting of the hunters was
quite distressing" was noted; one way of expressing the fact
of that ambiguity is to say that the sentence has two different meanings. Consider now the sentence "He has a pen"
and its French equivalent "Il a une plume." In those circumstances in which a speaker of English could properly use the
first, a speaker of French could properly use the second; each

4. Gottlob Frege, *The Basic Laws of Arithmetic,* trans. Montgomery
Furth (Berkeley and Los Angeles: University of California Press,
1964), p. 23.
5. Gottlob Frege, "On Sense and Reference," *Translations from the
Philosophical Writings of Gottlob Frege,* trans. Peter Geach and Max
Black (Oxford: Blackwell, 1952), p. 59. See also Rudolf Carnap, *The
Logical Syntax of Language* (New York: Humanities Press, 1951),
p. 42, and Ludwig Wittgenstein, *The Blue and Brown Books* (Oxford:
Blackwell, 1958), pp. 3-5.

could be used as a translation of the other. This fact of *translational equivalence* may be described by saying that the sentences have the same meaning. In these cases the notion of *sentence-meaning* is introduced to characterize certain undoubted aspects of language—ambiguity and translational equivalence. Whatever sentence-meaning is, it is at least something that different sentences can have in common and that the same sentence can have several of.

An objectivist account of meaning may use the notion of sentence-meaning in a special way. The phrase "the meaning of 'Il a une plume'" stands for a definite object that can be distinguished from other objects of the same type. For example, what it stands for is clearly different from what "the meaning of 'Il pleut'" stands for. Now, these objects cannot be identified with the sentences themselves; they are not linguistic entities at all, since sentences in different languages can have them in common. Let us call such objects *propositions*; let us say that a sentence expresses the proposition which is its meaning. When a sentence is ambiguous, then the proposition it expresses at a given time is the meaning it has at that time.

Thus far the switch from "meaning" to "proposition" is merely verbal. What else can be said about propositions to help us characterize the type of object they are? Let us note first of all that ordinary language does appear to have the means for forming names of propositions. If a speaker asserts that he has a pen, what he asserts is a certain proposition, and the phrase "that he has a pen" signifies it. In order to form the name of a proposition expressed by any sentences in English, preface the word "that" to the sentence.

Suppose one speaker, A, says "John has a pen," and another, B, thinks or believes that John has a pen. The very same thing that A asserted is also believed or thought by B. Since what A asserted is a proposition, then what B believed is also a proposition. Propositions, then, are not merely meanings of sentences but also objects of thought. This is a natural development of the theory of objective meanings because we use words to express our thoughts.

If it is true that John has a pen, then it is a *fact* that he has one. The locutions "it is true that . . ." and "it is a fact that . . ." seem to be equivalent, and what follows the words "true" and "fact" in each are names of propositions. It follows, then, that true propositions, in any case, can be plausibly identified with facts. Moreover, when we utter a sentence with the intention of asserting something true, then what we have done is to make a statement. When the sentence "John has a pen" is spoken, then the truth of the statement that John has a pen is asserted. It is *statements* that are asserted to be true or false. Asserting a fact and asserting a true statement seem to come to the same thing. It seems plausible to clarify the notion of proposition further by identifying propositions with the statements asserted in speaking certain sentences.

A Revision of the Theory

However plausible this approach appears to be, a false step has already been taken. Sentence-meanings and statements cannot be identified with each other because the relation between a sentence and its meaning and a sentence and the statement it is used to make are simply not the same. The following example illustrates this point: On March 3, A says, "It is now raining," and on June 5, B also says, "It is now raining." Since the sentence was not used ambiguously on the two occasions on which it was spoken, it was used on each occasion with the same meaning. But the statements made, though similar in content, are not exactly the same because they refer to different instances of rain. The statement made on March 3 could very well be true and the one made on June 5 false.[6]

Well, then, how are propositions to be characterized? Are they sentence-meanings or statements? The doubt can be resolved in the following way. When A spoke "It is now raining," he was both symbolizing a certain idea or content, the idea of rain occurring now, and simultaneously asserting the truth of that content. When a person makes a statement, there is a distinction to be drawn between what he does in speaking the sentence, namely, asserting something or other, and the something or other asserted, namely, the idea or content. Let us stipulate that propositions are to be classified as contents. They are things asserted or denied, not the assertions or denials themselves. But what about sentence-meanings? They cannot be identified as contents, since the content of the sentence "It is now raining" as spoken by A differs from the content of it when spoken by B. The difference is due to the fact that the word "now" refers to a different time on each occasion of use. If there were no difference in content, there would be no difference in the statements made. On the other hand, the content is not totally foreign to the meaning of the sentence. As a matter of fact, our understanding of the meaning of "It is now raining" consists in knowing the type of content or proposition that it can be used to assert. It is therefore plausible to identify the meaning of "It is now raining" with the content-type or propositional type it can be used to assert.

6. This argument obviously assumes that statements do not change their truth-value, that if T_1 is true and T_2 false, then $T_1 \neq T_2$. If this should be challenged, the reply is that the challenger is free to use the word "statement" differently, but that the argument does establish that statements, in the sense presupposed, are not to be identified with sentence-meanings.

But this is not yet quite accurate. Consider the sentences "It is now raining" and "Is it now raining?" They clearly have the same type of content or express the same type of proposition, namely, the idea of it's now raining, but since one is declarative and the other interrogative, they differ in meaning. Into the meaning of a sentence enters not only the content but also the type of *linguistic action* it can be used to perform. To specify the meaning of a sentence is to give both the appropriate type of action and the appropriate propositional type. Knowing these things enables us to interpret what is being said when the sentence is spoken on a particular occasion.

Propositions as Abstractions

Suppose that when A spoke "It is now raining" what he said was true and that when B said it his statement was false. At this point the theory of objective meanings comes to a fork in the road. According to one alternative, the sentence expresses the same proposition in each case, but its truth-value differs in relation to various contexts. Truth becomes relative to such contextual features as time, place, and speaker. Relative to a time and place at which it is raining the proposition expressed by "It is now raining" is true, and relative to a time and place at which it is not raining the proposition is false. There is no inconsistency in this alternative; there is no more a contradiction in saying that something is true relative to one factor and false relative to another than in saying that a given person is tall relative to the height of a mouse and short relative to the height of an elephant.

Although free from contradiction, such a view has several marks against it. First, it tends to tie the identity of propositions down to that of sentences—the same sentence, the same proposition. Yet this identity condition conflicts with one of the fundamental features of sentence-meaning, namely, that the same sentence can be used to convey different meanings. There is a further difficulty. Let us suppose that A spoke (1) "It is now raining" on March 3, 1967, in New York City. Whether or not such a sentence expresses a truth depends on where or when it is uttered. But the sentence (2) "It is raining on March 3, 1967, in New York City" has a truth capacity that is not dependent on the context.[7] Let us call the second sentence the *context-free counterpart* of the first. Given the resources of the English language and its contrivances for referring to places, times, and objects, almost every context-bound sentence has a context-free counterpart.[8] It is plausible to claim that (1) as spoken by A on March 13, 1967, in New York City says the same thing—asserts the same proposition—as (2). Now suppose that B also speaks (1), but on April 4, 1968, in Boston. Then the context-free counterpart of (1) as spoken by B is (3) "It is raining on April 4, 1968, in Boston." Clearly (2) and (3) express different propositions. But since (1) as spoken by B expresses the proposition expressed by (3), we could say not that the same proposition changes its truth-value, but rather that the same sentence expresses different propositions (of the same type) at different times and places.

If we accept this alternative, then propositions come to have an internal spatiotemporal reference and thus cannot be considered as entities that exist in space and time. The rain that falls exists in a certain place at a certain time; but that this rain falls at this place at this time is not itself a spatio-temporal thing. This is what is meant by the claim that propositions are abstract entities, where the abstract-concrete dichotomy is defined in terms of space-time locatability.

---

7. Provided that the copula "is" is interpreted timelessly as in "two plus two is four" rather than as a form of the present tense.

8. Exceptions might be sentences such as "It is now 10:00 P.M."

That propositions are abstract entities may not be thought to raise any problems, since they are, in a sense, perceptible. That it is now raining can be seen; its truth can be directly ascertained just by looking. But what about false propositions? They are not perceptible, since, being false, they are not facts that can be observed. The proposition expressed by a false sentence does not come under the scope of the senses.

Dispensing with Propositions

The various steps taken in developing and in modifying the theory of objective meanings may each seem plausible, but the dialectic finally arrives at a stage where it is necessary to call into question the existence of propositions themselves. The difficulty is not that propositions lack the tangibility of bodies, that they are not things that can be touched and seen. Rather, the fundamental problem is that by introducing the notion of propositions we are driven to a point at which it becomes mysterious and unintelligible how we can ever know the meaning of a sentence, particularly one that expresses something false. One of the champions of abstract entities has written:

> The extreme demand for a simple prohibition of abstract entities under all circumstances perhaps arises from a desire to maintain the connection between theory and observation. But the preference of (say) *seeing* over *understanding* as a method of observation seems to me capricious. For just as an opaque body may be seen, so a concept may be understood or grasped.[9]

9. Alonzo Church, "The Need for Abstract Entities in Semantic Analysis," reprinted in *The Structure of Language*, ed. Jerry Fodor and Jerrold Katz (Englewood Cliffs, N.J.: Prentice-Hall, 1964), p. 442.

According to this view, when a person hears someone speak
a sentence that he understands, not only does he observe the
sentence by his sensory mechanisms—that is, he hears it—but
he also observes its meaning—the proposition it expresses—
by means of some other type of mechanism. However, the
presumption that there is a parallel between sensory and non-
sensory modes of observation is mistaken. When sensory
methods of observation—seeing, hearing, touching, tasting,
and smelling—are under investigation, the nature, structure,
and function of the sense organs that form the physical basis
of these methods and the nature of the stimulus transmitted
from the observed object to the organ are relevant topics for
discussion. Inquiries may be undertaken to determine how
this stimulus is received by the organ, how the organ processes the stimulus and transmits the information it contains
to the brain, and how the brain responds to the nerve im-
pulses it receives. But, so far as we can now ascertain through
methods of psychological and physiological investigations,
there is no analogous organ adapted to observing propositions nor any stimulus that propositions transmit. Thus the
supposition that understanding is a method of observation,
a way of becoming aware of some entity that exists independently of the awareness of it, seems to be an ad hoc invention
designed to save the theory of objective meanings. If a theory
has much to recommend it and if it is clearly superior in
numerous ways to alternative accounts of the same phenomena,
then there is some justification in using ad hoc hypotheses to
adjust it to a few recalcitrant facts. But in our discussion so
far, no basis has yet been formulated on which to recommend
the theory of objective meanings over alternative accounts.
No alternatives have even been considered. Any theory chosen
to be investigated must explain and clarify the very same
phenomena that the theory of objective meanings was con-
structed to explain and to clarify. These phenomena were

sentence-ambiguity and translational equivalence. The initial step in the explanation was to form the hypothesis that there is such a thing as sentence-meaning, and this led us to the notion of propositions. It is time to subject this hypothesis to critical scrutiny.

2   Sentence-Use

Sentence-Meaning

Even though it is controversial how the notion of sentence-meaning is to be interpreted, its existence may seem obvious. A sentence is printed in a book; it makes good sense to ask, "What does that sentence mean?" and we know very well how to go about answering that question. So, the inevitable conclusion is that sentence-meanings must exist. Yet, as it stands, this argument is a faulty piece of metaphysics. To see the fallacy, let us consider the following case: In his notebook, A writes, "The shooting of the hunters was quite distressing." B asks, "What does that sentence mean?" The reason why B asks the question is that he has noted the ambiguity, and nothing in the context tells him which way the sentence is to be taken. The question is intended to elicit from A a clue as to how to interpret the sentence. When a speaker intends his words to be taken in a certain way, then he means something or other by his words. This concept of meaning is identical with that of the speaker's intention or the speaker's meaning. The fact that someone means something in speaking a sentence does not necessarily imply that the sentence has a meaning in its own right. A question that verbally appears to be a request for an explanation of the meaning of a sentence can often be interpreted as a request for the speaker's intention. So the mere fact that we can sensibly ask and answer, "What does that sentence mean?" fails to prove the reality of sentence-meanings.

One might claim that this argument shows that sentences do have meanings in the sense that people mean things when they speak them—that is, that sentence-meaning is reducible to speaker's intentions. Although this is a benign claim so far as it goes, it fails to accomplish one of the objectives that theories of sentence-meaning have set for themselves, namely, to explain in terms of the meanings sentences have why speakers choose the sentences they do in order to realize their intentions.

This criticism of the notion of sentence-meaning may appear to be vulnerable to the following response: The reason why B was in doubt about A's intention is that the sentence A spoke is, independently of his intention, susceptible to alternative interpretations; what B wanted to know was which of these interpretations was the one intended; to ascribe alternative interpretations to the sentence is to say that it has different meanings. If, however, the source of B's doubt is located more precisely, this response can be seen to be quite futile. What is ambiguous about the sentence is that the phrase "the shooting of the hunters" may be interpreted as exemplifying either of two distinct grammatical constructions. One is an action-object construction derived from "The hunters were shot," and the other is an agent-action construction derived from "The hunters were shooting."[1] B is not in doubt about some global feature of the sentence, such as its meaning, but about some special feature, namely, the grammatical structure of a phrase. Usually, doubts about what a speaker means or intends that are produced by ambiguity can be resolved by clarifying the grammar of a sentence or of its parts or by explaining the dictionary meaning of words in the sentence. There is, so far, no reason to employ the global notion of sentence-meaning in analyzing sentence-ambiguity.

Many of those who find a use for the notion of sentence-meaning assume that the meaning of any given sentence is

---

1. See Noam Chomsky's discussion of this phrase in his *Syntactic Structures* (The Hague: Mouton, 1963), pp. 88-89.

in some way composed out of the meanings of the separate
words that make up the sentence. For example, C. I. Lewis
says, "The meaning of any complex expression is a resultant
of the meaning of its elementary constituents together with
the syntactic relations of these in the whole expression."[2]
It is easy to see how such a view could be interpreted as an
argument in favor of the existence of sentence-meanings. If
what someone understands when he hears or reads a sentence
is something built up out of the meanings of the constituent
words together with their syntactic relations, then, it is in-
ferred, what he understands is the meaning of the sentence
as a whole; something built up out of parts that have meaning must itself have meaning.

This argument, however, is a good example of the fallacy
of composition—the fallacy of inferring from the fact that
each of the parts of a certain whole has a given property
that the whole has this property as well. From the fact that
each of the words in a sentence is short, it obviously does
not follow that the sentence is a short one. Similarly, from
the fact that each of the words in a sentence has meaning,
it does not follow that the sentence as a whole has meaning.
Again, however, an advocate of this type of argument may
adopt the strategy of reductionism: to say that a sentence
has meaning is just to say that it is a grammatically correct
construction from words each of which has meaning. Although this reductionist claim is similarly benign, it makes

2. C. I. Lewis, *An Analysis of Knowledge and Valuation* (La Salle,
Ill.: Open Court, 1946), p. 82. In his *The Philosophy of Language*
(New York: Harper & Row, 1966), p. 152, Jerrold Katz makes a
similar claim with respect to the process of interpreting sentences:
"The process by which a speaker interprets each of the infinitely
many sentences is a compositional process in which the meaning of
any syntactically compound constituent of a sentence is obtained
as a function of the meanings of the parts of the constituent."

the notion of sentence-meaning unimportant and theoretically superfluous; one could just as well jettison the concept altogether.

What shall we now say about the various arguments previously considered, upon which the theory of propositions relied? In general, these arguments stressed the fact that different sentences can have something in common or can resemble one another in various striking ways. Even if this common feature or point of resemblance is not to be identified with a proposition, certainly, one might argue, it can be identified with the meaning of a sentence. On the other hand, a careful examination of these crucial points of resemblance demonstrates that they can readily be described without introducing sentence-meanings at all. For example, instead of claiming that what the sentences "The door is closed," "Is the door closed?" and "Close the door!" have in common is their content or meaning, we can simply point out that each of them contains certain words in common—"door," "close," "the," that each of the words is used with the same meaning in all three of the sentences, and that each sentence combines the same words in a distinct grammatical construction. What "Brutus killed Caesar" and "Caesar was killed by Brutus" have in common is that the second is the passive transformation of the first and that each can be used to make the same statement. Finally what "I am hungry" and "J'ai faim" have in common is that their corresponding words as they occur in the sentence agree in meaning and/or function and that both can be used to make the same statement. From this point of view the notion of sentence-meaning thus appears superfluous.

Sentence-Use and Sentence-Meaning

There is another track that defenders of the notion of sentence-meaning have traveled, which stresses the significance of the fact that sentences are used in the performance of linguistic actions. For example, the sentence "I am hungry" can be used by speakers of English to make the same type of statement that "J'ai faim" can be used to make by speakers of French. It is plausible to formulate this point by saying that the first sentence has the same use in English as does the second in French. Whenever different sentences are found to possess the same or similar meanings, they turn out to have the same or similar uses. The sentence "The shooting of the hunters was quite distressing" can be used to make two different statements, and this difference in use corresponds to the point of ambiguity. It seems reasonable to infer that the meaning of a sentence is just its use in linguistic action. This identification of meaning with use avoids positing abstract entities such as propositions. Moreover, the notion of *sentence-use* is a global feature of sentences, which does not appear to be theoretically redundant—it is not reducible to the uses of the words that make up the sentence.[3]

That sentences are used is obvious; they are spoken in order to make statements, ask questions, give orders, and so forth. But it does not follow that sentences have a use. Not everything that something is used for is a use of that thing. A person may use a stick to ward off a threatening dog; but warding off dogs is not a use of the stick or of sticks in general. A hammer may be used as a paperweight, but that is not its use.

With respect to the notion of having a use, there seems to be a fundamental difference between words and sentences. A word can be used over and over again in different

3. For a theory of this sort see William Alston, *The Philosophy of Language* (Englewood Cliffs, N.J.: Prentice-Hall, 1964), p. 39.

sentences; it has a role or function. But it is doubtful whether sentences have a role or function in the same way. This has been noted by Gilbert Ryle.

> If I know the meaning of a word or phrase . . . I have learned to use the word correctly in an unlimited variety of different settings. . . . But the idea of putting a sentence to its work anywhen and anywhere is fantastic. It has not got a role which it can perform again and again in different ways. It has not got a role at all.[4]

Perhaps the difference between words and sentences that Ryle is trying to identify can be explained by reference to the following fact about language: when a person learns a language, he learns a finite number of words, which he uses over and over again to construct sentences; however, he seldom repeats the same sentence, and even those sentences that he occasionally does repeat do not occur with the same frequency.[5] A word is like an instrument that can be used over and over again for the same purpose; while sentences, although used to fulfill human purposes, are seldom used repeatedly. A series of sounds becomes a word in a language through repetition; without being used over and over again by numerous speakers a sound would fail to become established as a word in a spoken language. Repetition

4. Gilbert Ryle, "Ordinary Language," in *Philosophy and Ordinary Language,* ed. Charles Caton (Urbana, Ill.: University of Illinois Press, 1963), pp. 120-21.
5. This point is emphasized by Fodor and Katz: "The striking fact about the use of language is the absence of repetition—almost every sentence uttered is uttered for the first time. This can be substantiated by checking texts for the number of times a sentence is repeated. It is exceedingly unlikely that even a single repetition of a sentence of reasonable length will be encountered" ("The Structure of a Semantic Theory," reprinted in their *The Structure of Language,* p. 482).

is thus an essential feature of words. But that a sentence has been used before is not essential, is in fact irrelevant, to its being a sentence of the language and to its being understood by speakers of the language. This difference between words and sentences with respect to the significance of repetition marks one way in which words have uses while sentences do not. Since prior occurrences of a given sentence have nothing to do with its having meaning, sentence-meaning cannot be identified with this type of use.

Sentence-Use and Linguistic Action

There is, however, a different kind of use that is relevant to the topic of sentence-meaning. When a person speaks, unless his speech is idle, he performs certain linguistic actions. Linguistic actions are actions accomplished with words; when a person utters a sentence, we can ask, "What is he doing in speaking that sentence?" The answer will mention a certain linguistic act—he is making a certain statement or asking a certain question, and so forth.

Although sentences are linguistic means for the performance of actions, they do not work in exactly the same way that tools or instruments, such as a hammer or a saw, work in helping to perform certain actions. One difference is that a tool exists prior to the action and usually survives it, while a sentence may come into existence simultaneously with its being used as a means to an end and may never be used again. But however extensive the differences between tools and sentences, there is at least this analogy: speakers select sentences to accomplish actions they have in mind. Moreover, they select sentences in a nonarbitrary way: for example, if a speaker of English wishes to make the statement that it is now raining, it is more reasonable for him to select "It is raining" than "It is snowing." We can compare sentences with respect to the reasonableness of speaking them if a certain action is to be accomplished, and this comparison has nothing to do with their familiarity or the frequency of repetition. That familiarity and frequency are irrelevant to such a comparison can be demonstrated by this example: For someone who wishes to state that the purple bird is flying upside down around the plum tree, it is more reasonable for him to use the sentence "The purple bird is flying upside down around the plum tree" than "The yellow ostrich flies upside down under the pine tree."

How can we tell, when a sentence is spoken or written, what linguistic actions it is being used to perform? There are two kinds of cases to consider. The first is where we have no knowledge at all of the language to which the sentence belongs. For example, suppose that there is a sentence which we transcribe as "glickspill," which is spoken when and only when the speaker is pointing at an elephant. With this knowledge of the context of utterance, we have reason to believe that "glickspill" is spoken in order to state that there is an elephant in the vicinity. We do not as yet know the grammatical and semantic structure (the G-S structure) of "glickspill"; that is, we do not yet know how to break it down into individual words and morphemes, or what those hypothetical words individually mean, or how those words combine to make a correct sentence in the language. Thus we do not know what portion, if any, of "glickspill" corresponds to "elephant." The second kind of case is where we do know the language and therefore do not have to rely to the same extent upon the context in which the sentence is uttered. Thus, in order to know what is being said by "There is an elephant" we do not have to know that it is usually said only when there is an elephant in the vicinity. The G-S structure of sentences provides reasons for judging which actions they are used to perform.

What precisely is the relation between the G-S structure

and the action? Is knowing the first sufficient for knowing the second? The existence of sentence-ambiguity appears to be a reason for replying to the second question in the negative. Because "The shooting of the hunters was quite distressing" is ambiguous, it appears that we cannot tell merely from its G-S structure what it is being used to say. This is a shallow response, however. The fact of ambiguity establishes that this is a case where the "same" sentence can exemplify distinct, though overlapping, G-S structures, each structure corresponding to one way of removing the ambiguity. We can, consequently, reformulate the question as, What is the relation between a sentence with respect to one of its G-S structures and the action that it is used to perform or that it is reasonable for it to be used to perform? According to J. L. Austin, when a sentence is used on a given occasion to perform a certain linguistic action, it is thereby spoken with a certain *illocutionary force.* For example, if "Shut the door" is used to order someone to shut the door, it has the force of an order. If it is used as a request, then its utterance has the force of a request. Austin wished to distinguish between what a sentence means and the force with which it is spoken on a given occasion.

> Admittedly we can use "meaning" also with reference to illocutionary force—"He meant it as an order," etc. But I want to distinguish *force* and meaning in the sense in which meaning is equivalent to sense and reference.[6]

His basic argument for both distinguishing between meaning and force and establishing the absence of a correspondence between them consists of the citation of examples in which a sentence is used with different forces.

6. J. L. Austin, *How to Do Things with Words* (Oxford: Clarendon Press, 1962), p. 100.

It may be perfectly clear what I mean by "It is going to charge" or "Shut the door," but not clear whether it is meant as a statement or warning, etc. . . .

. . . We may agree on the actual words that were uttered, and even also on the senses in which they were being used and on the realities to which they were being used to refer, and yet still disagree as to whether, in the circumstances, they amounted to an order or a threat or merely to advice or a warning.[7]

The significance of Austin's examples may be diminished by scrutinizing more carefully the notion of a sentence. When the words "It is raining" are pronounced with a rising intonation, they are being used to ask a question; when pronounced with a falling intonation, they yield a statement. Intonation is a device whose effects can often be achieved in other ways. Thus if we change the word order to "Is it raining?" we have a form that clearly corresponds to a question. Suppose now we think of the intonation and stress as being part of the G-S structure of a sentence.[8] To consider one of Austin's cases, the words "Shut the door" could be pronounced differently depending upon whether they were used as a request or as a command. In that case the sentence would have two distinct G-S structures, and there would therefore be a correspondence between structure and act.[9]

7. Ibid., pp. 98, 114-15.

8. For a similar point see L. J. Cohen, "Do Illocutionary Forces Exist?", *Philosophical Quarterly* 14 (April 1964): 125-26. The rising intonation of an utterance of "It is raining" belongs to its syntactic structure just as much as the word order of "Is it raining?" which indicates that it is of interrogative form.

9. According to John Lyons, *Introduction to Theoretical Linguistics* (Cambridge: Cambridge University Press, 1969), modern linguists accept "the principle of the priority of the spoken language over the written" (p. 38). One of the reasons he cites is that "no

The actual facts are, however, more complex than a simple correspondence allows for. There are circumstances in which "Shut the door" has the force of a command even if it is pronounced in the same way as when it is used as a request. In the case of a general saying it to a private, for example, the force is determined not solely by the G-S structure, but also by the status and authority of the speaker. A mother says to her child in a statement-making tone of voice; "It is now 10:00 P.M."; the child, knowing his mother's intentions and expectations, takes it as a request for him to go to bed.

Actually, in many cases, the G-S structure of a sentence is a sufficient indication of the linguistic act being performed. In other cases it is necessary to pay attention to factors within the context of utterance, such as the intentions and authority of the speaker. Such contextual factors could not, by any stretch of the imagination, be thought of as being constituents of the G-S structure of the sentence. In addition, whether the force of a sentence is, in any given case, determined solely by the G-S structure or by a combination of structure and context, has nothing to do with the inherent nature of language. We can conceive of languages in which it was required that the illocutionary force of a sentence be explicitly symbolized, say, by a prefix. Instead of "Close the door," we would have "I order you to close the door" or "I request you to close the door," depending upon the act intended. For such languages, the G-S structure would be a sufficient mark of the linguistic action performed. At the other extreme, there could be a language in which the force was always indicated by some extrinsic factor, say a

---

writing-system represents all the significant variations of pitch and stress which are present in spoken utterances" (p. 40). If these significant variations are to be included within the G-S structure of a sentence, then this supports the principle that written language conveys syntactic structure less precisely than spoken language.

system of hand signals. Thus instead of "The door is closed," "Is the door closed?" and "Close the door," we could have, say, "close door" accompanied by the appropriate signal. Our actual languages are a combination of these extremes, sometimes relying upon explicit verbal signs and at other times relying upon extrinsic contextual factors. Thus, there is no simple correspondence between G-S structure and linguistic act, although it is always possible to create one.

Let us refer to a sentence with respect to any one of its G-S structures as a *sentence-interpretation*. Thus for "The shooting of the hunters was quite distressing," there are (at least) two sentence-interpretations. On the basis of the discussion so far, it is wrong to say that for each sentence-interpretation, there exists one and only one linguistic action.[10] On the other hand, if we know the interpretation under which a sentence is spoken or written, we thereby know the kinds of action it can be used to perform and those it cannot. Where there is no exact correspondence, then it is necessary to supplement knowledge of the sentence-interpretation with a grasp of contextual factors in order to determine all the things that are being said. We know that "Close the door" can be used to perform a variety of distinct though related actions– ordering, commanding, and requesting—but not stating or questioning. And because its interpretation limits its use in these ways, it is reasonable

10. There is, of course, a question as to the specific identity of linguistic acts. When A and B each say "I am hungry," are they each saying the same thing? The word "I" refers to a different person in each case. So in one sense of "statement" they are making different statements. But in another sense they are saying the same thing, that is, they are making the same type of statement. In this discussion, it is the *type* of linguistic act that is important, and by a type is meant a classification in which the two utterances of A and B belong to the same type, whereas when C says, "She is hungry," what he says does not belong to that type.

for speakers to use it to perform the permitted acts in order
to be understood. Even a sentence fragment such as "Yes"
provides an indication that the speaker is responding to some
previous question or request even though the content re-
sponded to is not given.

The fact that sentences can be spoken under interpretations
which limit the actions that can reasonably be made with
them determines which sentences speakers select in the attempt to communicate to others. It may be necessary to
know certain contextual factors in order to identify the
interpretation with which the sentence is uttered, and once
the interpretation has been identified, it may be necessary
to employ further contextual factors to identify the action.
For example, if A says to a group of people "Raise your
arms," until we know whether "arms" here designates a
part of the body or a weapon, we have not fixed the interpretation. Furthermore, once that is determined, we do not
know whether the action was a request or a command until
we know the status of A with respect to those he is address-
ing.

In one sense of "use" it is reasonable to call this feature
of sentences their use. A *sentence-use* thus consists of the
capacity of one of its interpretations to be used to perform
some acts and not others, depending upon its G-S structure.[11]
For each sentence-interpretation there is, thus, one and only
one use, but each use may correspond to more than one
linguistic action. This concept of use is not susceptible to
Ryle's criticism that "the idea of putting a sentence to its
work anywhen and anywhere is fantastic. It has not got a
role that it can perform again and again. It has not got a

---

11. A sentence-use is similar to what Alston calls an illocutionary
act potential. See *The Philosophy of Language*, p. 39.

role at all." Perhaps in the way in which Ryle was using "role," sentences do not have roles. But clearly they do have uses. For a sentence to have a use it is not necessary that it be uttered "again and again" or ever uttered at all.[12]

It is certainly plausible to identify sentence-meaning and sentence-use. Just as sentences can have different meanings, so by having distinct interpretations, they can have different uses. Just as different sentences can have the same meaning, so they can have the same use.[13] This concept of sentence-meaning, like the others we have recently examined, is theoretically eliminable, since it is explicated in terms of the notions of sentence-interpretation (and thus of G-S structure) and of linguistic action. But just because it is a concept that represents connections between these notions, it is not made useless by being shown to be eliminable.

---

12. The notion of sentence-use applies to types, not to tokens.

13. On this view there is a distinction to be drawn between a sentence's meaning and the illocutionary force (or linguistic act) with which it is spoken on a given occasion, even though the definition relates the two concepts. For a critique of Austin that attempts to identify meaning with force see Cohen, "Do Illocutionary Forces Exist?" In the case where the force was always explicitly represented in the sentence, say, by some kind of prefix, then to each use there would correspond one and only one force, and hence force could be identified with meaning.

3 Linguistic Action

Performatives

On the basis of the discussion thus far, we can claim that the notion of linguistic action is theoretically more fundamental than that of sentence-meaning. The meaning of a sentence is its capacity, given an interpretation, to occur in certain linguistic actions. In this and in the following sections the concept of a linguistic action, an action performed with words, will become the primary subject of discussion. Initially, we shall pay some attention to a concept first introduced by J. L. Austin, the notion of a *performative*. Austin identified the concept and illuminated it with a wealth of illustrations, but because he tended to think that the concept was defective in a fundamental way, he neglected to develop it systematically.[1]

In what follows, the existence of a standard context of communication will be assumed: it contains a speaker S and a listener(s) L both belonging to the same language community; S says something to L; L is receptive and attentive to what S says; S is not interested in misleading L about his intentions or beliefs. When we say that S speaks or utters a sentence, the terms "speech" and "utterance" will be used more broadly than is customary, to designate written as well as spoken sentences. When a sentence is spoken, either in speech or in writing, a physical realization of it is produced consisting either of a series of sounds in the one case

1. For Austin's theory of performatives see his *How to Do Things with Words* and his two articles "Performative Utterances" (in his *Philosophical Papers* [Oxford: Clarendon Press, 1961], pp. 220-39) and "Performative-Constative" (in Caton, ed., *Philosophy and Ordinary Language*).

or written marks in the other. Such marks or sounds will be called an *inscription* of the sentence.

I shall develop my view of performatives by using as an example an action of promising. In particular, S promises L to return a book he has borrowed by saying, "I promise to return the book soon." The following distinctions are relevant: First, there is the distinction between the sentence that S speaks and S's act of speaking it. The same sentence may be spoken by different speakers at different times. Second, there is the distinction between the sentence and the action of promising. The sentence is the linguistic means chosen by S to perform the action. Third, it is necessary to distinguish between the act of speaking the sentence and the action of promising; they are distinct actions, the latter being the result of the former, and the one could have occurred without the other—S could have made that promise without speaking that sentence, and he could have uttered the sentence without succeeding in making the promise.

The features of this example that are distinctive of performatives are: (1) In the appropriate circumstances, the speaking of the sentence is sufficient for the act of promising to be made. That is what makes promising a linguistic action—an action accomplished by means of words despite the fact that one can describe the action without mentioning words. (2) In speaking the sentence, S is not stating or asserting that he is promising; he is simply promising. In this respect a sentence beginning with "I promise" is different from one starting with "He promises." (3) The sentence contains the word "promise," which signifies the very action being accomplished.

A number of terms can be illustrated by reference to this example. The *performative action* is the linguistic action performed by speaking the sentence. There are various levels

of abstraction at which the action can be described. If the
action is described simply as an act of promising then what
is mentioned is a general performative action. If it is described
as the action of promising L to return the book soon, then
what is mentioned is the specific performative action. There
is, in addition, the *performative sentence* "I promise to return the book soon" and the *performative utterance,* which
is the action of speaking the performative sentence. Within
the sentence there are those words that signify or describe
the performative action: the *performative action description.* The description can be general such as "promise" or
specific such as "promise to return the book soon."

Take another example. S warns L to stay away from his
wife by saying, "I warn you to stay away from my wife."
The general performative action is warning, the specific
is warning L to stay away from his wife; the performative
sentence is "I warn you to stay away from my wife"; the
action of speaking this sentence is the performative utterance; and the performative act descriptions are "warn"
(general) and "warn you to stay away from my wife"
(specific).

Among performative actions are those typically accomplished
by the use of sentences beginning with the following phrases:
"I promise," "I warn," "I order," "I state," "I bet," I
apologize," "I choose," "I congratulate," "I implore,"
"I appoint," "I conclude," "I ask," and many others.
Each of these sentences is in the first-person singular, present tense; in most cases, if the tense or quantity or person
is changed, the utterance is no longer performative but becomes an assertion of the occurrence of the act indicated.
There are, however, exceptions; if "we" is substituted for
"I," and if the speaker is authorized to speak for the group,
there still can be a performative as in "We apologize. . . ."
In addition, many of these sentences have a passive trans-

formation that is still performative: "You are ordered," "You are asked," and so on. There are still other grammatical forms appropriate for the performative function; for example, "Trespassers are hereby warned. . . ." In the case of a performative action directed by the speaker at himself, such as "I resolve to stop smoking," S and L may be identical.

For Austin it was essential that performative utterances or actions be neither true nor false. Performatives for him were partly defined by contrasting them with statements that do have a truth-value.[2] It is not clear why he insisted on this point, but perhaps the reason is that since the performative action is not an assertion of its own existence, Austin concluded that it is not an assertion at all. Thus the action of promising made by a sentence beginning with "I promise" does not assert that a promise is being made; it is a promise. And in this case there is no assertion being made at all. That promising was, for Austin, a paradigm case of a performative further reinforced his conviction. He noticed, however, that when a person speaks a sentence beginning with "I state" or "I assert," he brings about an action, that is, he makes a statement or an assertion. And except for the fact that such statements have a truth-value, they are in every other way like performatives. Instead of dropping the requirement that performatives must lack a truth-value, Austin dropped the notion of a performative entirely and turned to the more general notions of speech act and illocutionary force.[3] In the approach

2. Thus in introducing the notion of a performative he writes: "I want to discuss a kind of utterance which looks like a statement and grammatically, I suppose, would be classed as a statement, which is not nonsensical, and yet is not true or false" (Austin, "Performative Utterances," p. 222).

3. Ibid., p. 238.

to performatives adopted here, the requirement of lacking a
truth-value will be dropped because it is perfectly arbitrary.
Performative actions are subject to various sorts of evaluation,
as Austin noted: orders can be wise or stupid, a promise can
be prudent or rash, and a statement can be true or false.
There is no special reason to single out the truth-value as
somehow demarcating performatives from nonperformatives.

A rough definition of the notion of a performative utterance is as follows: S's speaking a sentence T is a performative
utterance provided—

(1) the circumstances are appropriate for his doing a
specific action A by his uttering T
(2) S utters T in order to do A
(3) T contains a phrase W used in that utterance by S
to signify the action he intends to perform by his
uttering T
(4) S does not intend his uttering T to be the assertion
that he is doing A.

A is the performative action, T the performative sentence,
and W the performative action description. The reason for
clause (1) in the definition is that in order for the utterance
to be sufficient for the action, the circumstances must be
appropriate. In the case of S's promising to return the book
to L, in order for his utterance to result in a promise, then
it must be true that L lent the book to S, that L expects it
back, and that L hears S's words. The type of circumstance
that is appropriate will vary from performative to performative. The reason for (2) is that idle speech is not performative;
the performative action must be the reason why T is spoken.
Clause (3) represents the distinctive feature of performatives,
namely, that they refer to the action performed without
asserting that it is performed. Of course, this does not pre-
vent some other action from being asserted as in, "I state

that I am writing." The reason for (4) is peripheral; it is designed to exclude certain types of cases. If S should say, "I am promising to return the book," and if he intends and understands his utterance to be the making of a promise, then the utterance satisfies (1), (2), and (3), but it is not a performative in the strict sense because it also asserts the existence of the act of promising.

Suppose S says to L, "I convince you that p," where p is a statement that S wants to persuade L to believe. This is a strange sentence to utter, and perhaps S made some kind of error. But, assuming that it is a grammatical sentence at all, then it is possible that its utterance is performative according to our definition: (1) the circumstances may, in some way, be appropriate for S to convince L that p; (2) S may believe that L is credulous and liable to believe anything S says, so that uttering this sentence may have the effect of convincing L that p; (3) the sentence contains a phrase "convince you that p," which indicates which action S intends to perform; and (4) the utterance need not be the assertion that S is convincing L.

But clearly something is wrong here. Whether or not L is convinced is not solely up to S's uttering the appropriate words. Convincing L is an effect of S's linguistic action and not a linguistic action itself. The idea of a performative action is that it is something a speaker can do all by himself merely by uttering a sentence, assuming the circumstances are appropriate. It is not something that waits upon the effects of his utterance on the audience. Austin noted this point when he distinguished between an *illocutionary act,* which is a speech act of which peformatives are a species, and a *perlocutionary act,* which is the effect of the speech act. Often we refer to the effects of our own actions as if these were our actions themselves. We can speak of a person being convinced or of our convincing him, of a person being mollified or our mollifying him. Even when we ascribe the action to ourselves, its existence depends upon the effects of what we do upon others. But a performative act is not dependent in this way. Of course, certain facts about others are often part of the circumstances that make it appropriate to perform the act just by uttering words; for example, for a promise to be made the hearer must actually hear the promise. Hearing the promise is in a sense an effect of the performative utterance. But it is an effect that properly belongs to the context that makes it reasonable to utter those words. The perlocutionary act is something postcircumstantial; it is an effect simpliciter, not one belonging to the circumstances or context of the act in the sense intended.

If we interpret the preceding definition of performative utterance in the light of these considerations, then we see that the utterance of "I convince you that p" is not and cannot be a performative utterance. In the sense of "appropriate circumstances" we have in mind in clause (1), the circumstances cannot be appropriate for S's convincing L merely by his uttering "I convince you that p." Rather, whether he succeeds in convincing L depends upon the postcircumstantial effects of the utterance on L and is not solely up to him and the circumstances. To make this qualification explicit in the definition, we should reformulate (1) to read: "the background circumstances are appropriate for his directly bringing about a specific action A merely by his uttering T."

Austin hinted at different ways of handling this problem. He tended to identify the performative act with the performative utterance. "The issuing of the utterance is the performing of an action. . . . The idea of a performative utterance was that it was to be (or be included as a part of) the performance of an action."[4] If promising to return the book

4. Austin, *How to Do Things with Words*, pp. 6, 60.

is, in the appropriate circumstances, the very same action as uttering the sentence "I promise to return the book," then there is no difficulty in principle in distinguishing the consequences of the performative act from the action itself; everything that is a consequence of the utterance is also other than the performative action. Rather than adopt this approach, I have been viewing the performative action as a result of the utterance and not as identical with it. My justification is that this definition accords with our actual ways of speaking and thinking. We say that S promised L by means of the sentence "I promise to return the book to you." We say that S made the promise by uttering this particular sentence, but he could have made it by saying something else.

Austin suggests another means of dealing with the distinction between linguistic action and perlocutionary consequences. The linguistic or illocutionary action is one done according to conventions; it is a conventional action, whereas the perlocutionary action is a real effect and not a conventional one.

> The consequential effects of perlocutions are really consequences, which do not include such conventional effects as, for example, the speaker's being committed by his promise (which comes into the illocutionary act). . . . There is clearly a difference between what we feel to be the real production of real effects and what we regard as mere conventional consequences.[5]

Austin, however, never makes his concept of convention quite clear. Moreover, if speech is regulated by linguistic conventions, then there are perlocutionary consequences of linguistic actions that are as conventional as linguistic

5. Ibid., p. 102.

actions simply because they are linguistic acts themselves:
for example, L responds, "I will not" to S's, "I order you
to close the door."

Quasi Performatives

A performative action was defined as an action that comes
about through a performative utterance. Such actions can
also be brought about in other ways; for example, an order
may be communicated by a gesture, an assertion by a nod.
Performativeness is not an intrinsic but a relational feature
of actions. An action is performative relative to its being
the consequence of a certain utterance by a certain person
at some definite time. The same action done by someone
else may not be performative at all.

Actions that are brought about by performative utterances can usually also be accomplished by utterances that
are not performative. S can order L to shut the door not
merely by saying, "I order you to shut the door," but also
by, "Shut the door." This is not a performative utterance,
since it fails to satisfy clause (3) of the definition. For example, S can promise to return the book merely by saying,
"I will return the book"; he can assert that two plus three
is five merely by saying, "Two plus three equals five," but
neither of these are performatives. I shall stipulate, therefore, that an utterance which can have the same result as
a performative but whose sentence lacks a general performative action description is a *quasi-performative utterance*. It is obvious that a great proportion of our speech—
all statements, commands, questions, requests, and so
forth—consists either of performatives or of quasi performatives. The actions that are the results of issuing quasi
performatives will also be called performative actions. It
is obvious from the definition that whatever performative
action can be accomplished by issuing a quasi performative

can also be accomplished by a performative utterance. Let us refer to this relationship as the reducibility of quasi performatives to performatives.

Since what we say is often communicated implicitly by context as well as conveyed explicitly by speech, how we perform any particular reduction depends not merely on the sentence uttered but on extrinsic circumstances. Suppose S says to L, "I know that two plus three equals five." We know, let us suppose, that S intends not merely to assert an autobiographical fact about his own knowledge but also to assert the arithmetical fact itself and to assure or guarantee L of the truth of what he claims to know. In reduced form, then, S's quasi performative comes to: "I state that two plus three equals five, and I state that I know that two plus three equals five, and I assure you that two plus three equals five." It is clear that the need for quasi performatives is founded in part on their brevity.

In the performative sentence "I promise to return the book to you soon," we can distinguish the term indicating the agent who does the performative action, namely, "I," the term mentioning the type of action, namely, "promise," and the term indicating the specific content of the performative act, namely, "to return the book to you soon." These are, respectively, the *agent description,* the general performative action description, and the *content description.* In "I ask you whether two plus three equals five," the agent description is "I," the action description is "ask," and the content description is "whether two plus three equals five." In "Trespassers are hereby warned to keep off" there is no agent indicator. In "I warn you" there is no content description. If the utterance is a genuine performative, there must always be an action description. Whenever one of the descriptions is absent, it is possible to issue another performative in which it is present. Let us call those performative utterances whose performative sentences contain all three descriptions *fully explicit performative utterances*. What I shall call the *idealized performative utterance* will simply be a standardized way of expressing a fully explicit performative. The idealized version consists of first the agent description, then the act description, and then the content description all in the form of an appropriate sentence. Here are some examples:

"I promise: I will return the book soon."
"I order: Close the door."
"I request: Close the door."
"I ask: Does two plus three equal five?"
"I apologize: I have been rude to you."
"I warn: Trespassers will be prosecuted."
"I congratulate: You have won the prize."

In each case the content description could be used in a quasi-performative utterance, and the idealized performative as a whole is something to which the quasi performative can be reduced. The idealized version allows us to represent perspicuously the relation between quasi performatives and forms to which they are reducible. The initial part of the idealized performative sentence, which consists of both the agent and the act descriptions, will be called the *performative operator*.

The Reducibility of Linguistic Actions

The question of whether all linguistic actions are reducible to performatives can be formulated in a variety of ways. If I put it one way, I am asking whether any action that can be performed by means of uttering words can also be performed as a performative act in which the words uttered take the form of a performative sentence. Since all per-

formatives have an idealized version, I am also asking
whether any utterance can be represented as an idealized
performative utterance. And since all quasi performatives
are reducible to performatives, I am asking whether all
utterances that are not performatives are quasi performatives.

Austin would have answered these questions in the negative.

> Is it always the case that we must have a performative
> verb for making explicit something we are undoubted-
> ly doing by saying something? For example, I may in-
> sult you by saying something, but we have not the
> formula "I insult you."[6]

Suppose S insults L by saying, "You are a fool." Austin is
claiming in effect that there is no idealized performative
utterance in English, such as "I insult: You are a fool," to
which "You are a fool" is reducible. His reason is that in
ordinary English the phrase "I insult" does not function
as a performative operator. There is, however, another way
of analyzing this example. The reason why "I insult" is not
a performative operator may be that insulting someone is
not a linguistic act at all but is rather a perlocutionary act,
that is, a consequence of a speech act. For suppose after S
says, "You are a fool," L replies, "I agree," and refuses to
be insulted. S tried but failed to insult him. After all, "You
are a fool" can be reduced to "I state: You are a fool." One
insults people by making statements about them that they
think are unpleasant and false; the existence of the insult
depends upon how the statement is taken. "I insult" can
no more be a performative operator than "I convince."

There are other cases about which Austin had doubts.

6. Ibid., p. 65. See also pp. 68-69.

> Suppose, for example, somebody says "Hurrah." Well,
> not true or false; he is performing the act of cheering.
> Does that make it a performative utterance in our sense
> or not? Or suppose he says "Damn"; he is performing
> the act of swearing, and it is not true or false. Does that
> make it performative? We feel that in a way it does and
> yet it's rather different.[7]

Despite these qualms, there is no difficulty in formulating
idealized versions of these examples—"I cheer: Hurrah,"
and "I swear: Damn." Similarly for "Ouch"—"I exclaim:
Ouch." Of course, we would seldom or never preface our
cheering by "I cheer" or our swearing by "I swear." In
these and many cases the quasi performative is clearly pre-
ferred to the fully explicit performative, and the performative operator is not used. This, however, is a linguistic
accident and hence, for our purposes, insignificant.

In addition to looking at particular cases, there is a general argument to support the claim that all linguistic actions are reducible to performatives. Let A be a linguistic
act, and let V be a verb signifying A. We can then formulate a performative operator in the usual way by taking V
in the first-person singular, present tense and forming a performative sentence by adding the appropriate content description. It is necessary, however, to make two qualifications
in the force of this argument. First, it might not be customary to perform A by means of a performative sentence; as
in the cases just mentioned, the quasi performative may be
more natural to use. What can be communicated by means
of the quasi performative therefore might not get across by
means of the fully explicit version. The reducibility thesis,
then, must not be interpreted to mean that performative

7. Austin, "Performative Utterances," p. 233.

sentences are always just as serviceable communicating devices as are quasi performatives. Second, it is logically possible that although a language contains the means for performing A, it might not contain a verb V signifying A. It is possible, for example, that English could fail to contain the verb "order" or any of its equivalents even though it contains the grammatical and semantic means to give orders. Given this abstract possibility, the reducibility thesis must now be formulated as: linguistic actions are reducible to performatives to just the extent that the language contains the appropriate verbs. But even if the appropriate verb should be absent, we could always invent one and introduce it into the language, so that this qualification is not crucial.

In general, then, any linguistic or illocutionary action can, in principle, be performed as a performative act by means of a performative sentence in explicit or idealized form. The theory of performatives thus suffices as a theory of linguistic acts.

4   Conventions

Conventions and Rules

It is generally agreed that certain of the fundamental features of language such as word-meaning and grammar are conventional or arbitrary. Though this agreement is widespread and of ancient origin, it is not clear what it amounts to. Austin, carrying on in this tradition, wished to assert that illocutionary acts are constituted by convention. Here are some passages from *How to Do Things with Words* that summarize his views:

> We must notice that the illocutionary act is a conventional act: an act done as conforming to a convention. [P. 105]

> The illocutionary act . . . has a certain *force* in saying something. . . . Illocutionary acts are conventional acts. [P. 120]

> There cannot be an illocutionary act unless the means employed are conventional. [P. 118]

> The act is constituted not by intention or by fact, essentially, but by *convention*. [P. 127]

> What we do import by the use of the nomenclature of illocution is a reference, not to the consequences (at least in any ordinary sense) of the locution, but to the conventions of illocutionary force as bearing on the special circumstances of the occasion of the issuing of the utterance. [P. 114]

Because Austin distinguished illocutionary force from meaning, we can assume that for him the conventions of illocutionary force are not to be identified with semantic conventions. In addition, conventions are here contrasted both with intentions and with facts. But Austin does not say anything further about the nature of convention, and his basic idea remains hidden in obscurity.

Let us consider the general question of the nature of conventions independently of language and then return to the case of language later on. As an example of a typical convention, I shall use the practice of greeting by shaking hands. Shaking hands is a conventional way of greeting in our culture. Whenever there is a conventional way of doing something for a group of persons, there exists a certain regularity that holds for those persons; in this case the regularity consists of the co-occurrence of shaking hands with occasions for greeting.[1] The co-occurrence of smoke with fire is also a regularity but not a conventional one. What, then, is the difference between the two regularities in virtue of which one is conventional and the other not? As an initial answer one might say that the latter is a causal regularity whereas the former is not. But in the absence of a specific analysis of causality, this answer will not do. Within that group in which the convention holds, greeting is a result of shaking hands just as smoke is a result of fire. Just as one can bring about smoke by making a fire, so one can bring about a greeting by shaking hands. Of course, in the case of greet-

1. A regularity may very well have exceptions. In his *Convention: A Philosophical Study* (Cambridge: Harvard University Press, 1969), David K. Lewis constructs an analysis of the notion of conventional regularity, which I have found useful in developing my own approach. Although Lewis's analysis does not make use of the notion of intention or purpose explicitly (see his final definition on p. 78), nevertheless he asserts (pp. 154-55) that it is implied.

ing, the effect is due to the conventional connection between cause and effect, whereas fire brings about smoke quite independently of human convention. So it is not the presence or absence of causality in a broad sense that constitutes the difference between the absence or presence of a convention.

There is a tradition in Western philosophy according to which conventions originate in human agreement, which distinguishes conventional from nonconventional regularities. Thus Hobbes has written:

> There are two kinds of signs; the one *natural*; the other done upon *agreement,* or by express or tacit composition. Now because in every language, the use of *words* and *names* comes by appointment, it may also by appointment be altered; for that which depends on and derives its force from the will of men, can by the will of the same men agreeing be changed again or abolished.[2]

If by "agreement" is meant something like a social contract, namely, a promise to participate on the condition that others do so as well or an explicit agreement expressed in signs, then clearly not every convention is the product of an agreement. In order for there to be a conventional regularity, it is obviously not necessary for there to have been an actual historical event in which the participants announced an agreement.

There is, however, another sense of "agreement," which is perhaps what Hobbes had in mind by the phrase "tacit

2. See Hobbes, *Selections,* p. 14n. In a similar vein, John Locke has written: "Thus we may conceive how *words* . . . came to be made use of by men as the signs of their *ideas*; not by any natural connection that there is between particular articulate sounds and certain *ideas,* for then there would be but one language amongst all men; but by a voluntary imposition, whereby such a word is made arbitrarily the mark of such an *idea*" (*An Essay Concerning Human Understanding,* bk. 3, chap. 2, par. 1).

composition." It is the sense in which David Hume uses the term when, after criticizing the social-contract theory of the origin of property, he goes on to say that property rights originate in human convention, and he gives the following illustration to make his meaning clear:

> Thus, two men pull the oars of a boat by a common convention for a common interest, without any promise or contract; thus, gold and silver are made the measures of exchange; thus, speech and words and language are fixed by human convention and agreement.[3]

In this context, that the meanings of words are fixed by agreement means nothing more than that persons agree in their use—that there are conventions of use. There is a difference between an agreement to do something and an agreement in doing something. But though it is the latter that is the relevant notion of agreement for the concept of convention, to refer to it is simply to restate that here we have a convention and is not to explain what a convention is.

Another theory explains conventions as being rules, or rather claims that speaking of rules is preferable to speaking of conventions at all. Thus William Alston has written:

> Like the social contract theory in political science, the idea that words get their meaning by convention is a myth if taken literally. But like the social contract theory, it may be an embodiment, in mythical form, of important truths that could be stated in more sober terms. It is our position that this truth is best stated in terms of the notions of rules. That is, what really demarcates symbols is the fact that they have what mean-

3. David Hume, *Enquiry Concerning the Principles of Morals*, app. 3.

ing they have by virtue of the fact that for each there
are rules in force, in some community, that govern their
use.[4]

The notion of a rule is not, as it stands, a very clear concept and may comprehend things that have no relevance to
our problems. One kind of rule is a conventional social practice; but to invoke this kind is not to explicate the notion
of convention but to substitute another word. Another kind
of rule is a regulation such as the prohibition against smoking in the theater; regulations are laid down by authorities
who have the right to promulgate them and to apply sanctions to those who violate them. An important class of regulations are the criminal laws that impose penalties on certain
forms of behavior. But neither the practice of shaking hands
nor the practice of using the word "red" to refer to the
color are regulations, since there is no identifiable authority
backing them nor specific sanctions accompanying their
violations.

There is a rather broad notion of a rule that has been invoked often in contemporary philosophy; it is the notion
that rules are standards of correct behavior enabling us to
distinguish between a right and wrong way of doing things.
Thus Peter Winch has written:

> The notion of following a rule is logically inseparable
> from the notion of *making a mistake*. If it is possible
> to say of someone that he is following a rule that means
> that one can ask whether he is doing what he does cor-
> rectly or not. . . . The point of the concept of a rule is
> that it should enable us to *evaluate* what is being done.

4. Alston, *The Philosophy of Language*, pp. 57-58.

In showing that a man is not following a rule, it is not conclusive to demonstrate that he cannot formulate it or say what it is.

> The test of whether a man's actions are the application of a rule is not whether he can *formulate* it but whether it makes sense to distinguish between a right and a wrong way of doing things in connection with what he does. Where that makes sense, then it must also make sense to say that he is applying a criterion in what he does even though he does not, and perhaps cannot, formulate that criterion.

Using this notion of a rule, Winch formulates a far-reaching thesis about human behavior: "All behaviour which is meaningful (therefore all specifically human behaviour) is *ipso facto* rule-governed."[5] If this notion of a rule is used to explain what a convention is, then it follows that in all specifically human behavior persons are following conventions whether they are aware of them or not.

Winch's general thesis is dubious. There are many kinds of mistakes that are not, in any ordinary sense, violations of rules or of conventions; for example, a man may fall off his bicycle or stumble while walking. Perhaps these behaviors would not be classed by Winch as being "specifically human." But for his general thesis to be informative and not merely tautological, he must define specifically human behavior in a way that does not invoke rules.

In any case, our problem is whether conventions are to be identified with standards of correct behavior. The practice of greeting by shaking hands could be thought of in this light. Shaking hands in our culture is the correct way

5. Peter Winch, *The Idea of a Social Science* (London: Routledge and Kegan Paul, 1963), pp. 32, 58, 52.

of greeting one another; failure to do so can often be labeled
as a type of incorrect behavior, as being thoughtless or rude
or hostile. But the question is not whether some conventions are standards of correct behavior but whether they
must be so. And it is obvious upon reflection that there is
no inherent necessity here. We can conceive of a permissive
culture in which persons habitually shake hands when greeting but which allows various kinds of alternative behaviors
at will and does not subject those who fail to go along with
the convention to criticism.

Let us consider a linguistic example. The sentence "The
men is home" is incorrect or ungrammatical; it violates, we
can say, a grammatical convention of the English language.
But does it go against a rule or standard of correct behavior?
Consider the following two formulations:

> (1) In English sentences with a plural subject, the
>   present-tense form of the verb "to be" that *should*
>   be used is "are," not "is."
> (2) Among speakers of English, sentences whose verb
>   is a present-tense form of "to be" contain "is" after
>   a singular third-person subject and "are" after a
>   plural.

Although (1) is formulated as a rule or a prescription, we can
think of (2) as a factual descriptive statement formulating a
statistically predominant usage among speakers of English.
Let us suppose, as is likely, that interpreted in this way (2)
turns out to be true. We can then come to understand how
the rule (1) comes to exist as a result of the truth of (2).
Certain persons in the language community—teachers, writers,
grammarians, and others—acquire an interest in preserving
certain existing linguistic practices, and, as a result, tend to
criticize those whose use is statistically deviant as speaking
incorrect English. As a result of training and indoctrination

in the community's educational system and as a result of the attitudes of adults, people come to feel that their use ought to conform to (2), and in this way the rule (1) comes into existence.

The purpose of this story of the evolution of (1) out of (2) is not to state the actual relation between them, although our account is probably the correct one, but merely to indicate that it is possible to have linguistic conventions without prescriptive rules or standards of correct behavior. We can understand that linguistic rules do serve a fundamental interest, for they help to maintain uniformity of usage and hence to maintain language as a vehicle of communication among different persons. This interest, though fundamental, is not logically indispensable. We can imagine situations in which an interest in and a need to distinguish between right and wrong usage diminishes, fades, or disappears altogether. We can imagine a culture that adopts a permissive view toward its symbolic systems; linguistic change, innovation, and diversity would be positively encouraged; persons would be urged to make changes, to explore the consequences of the changes they make, and to invent novel systems. As far as linguistic usage is concerned, in such a culture people would adopt the attitude: "This is what we do, but you should feel free to do something different if you wish." Members of the community would come to experience existing practices not as constraints binding upon them but as habitual ways of doing things to which there are alternatives. The members of such a community, if they allow this permissive attitude to go too far, may have to pay the price of increasing difficulty in understanding one another. But the point to note is that because it is possible to think away standards of correct linguistic behavior, it is not correct to analyze the notion of a convention as a rule.

Another illustration of this point is the continuing debate concerning the nature and function of dictionaries. One party to the debate believes that a dictionary should be a guide to correct usage, that the definitions of words should function as rules enabling one to distinguish between correct and incorrect usage. The other party insists that a dictionary should describe rather than prescribe usage, that its definitions should record statistically preponderant usage. The editor of one widely used dictionary advocates what he calls a "linguistically sound middle course"—to describe usage and also to describe "the attitudes of society toward particular words or expressions, whether he regards these attitudes as linguistically sound or not."[6] According to this view, the definitions do not themselves constitute rules but contain descriptions of rules without endorsing them. Thus in the entry for the word "ain't," this dictionary contains the comment: " 'Ain't' is so traditionally and widely regarded as a nonstandard form that it should be shunned by all who prefer to avoid being considered illiterate." Here one is not categorically advised to shun "ain't" but is informed that if one uses the term, one is in danger of being considered illiterate. The very possibility of having a purely descriptive dictionary implies that definitions need not be taken as standards of correct usage and that conventions are not to be identified with rules.

The dictionary example suggests that there are three ways of taking a formulation like (2). First, it may be taken simply as a description of predominant usage. Second, it may be interpreted as a rule in the sense that one who accepts (2) accepts it as a standard of correct usage on the basis of which he evaluates his own and others' speech. Or third, it may be taken as a description of the rules accepted by those who

6. Jess Stein, Preface to *The Random House Dictionary of the English Language* (New York: Random House, 1966), p. vi.

speak English. Someone who accepts (2) in this third way is not merely asserting a statistical generalization, although this is implied, and he is not committing himself to the rule; he is asserting that speakers of English accept it as a rule. This is the standpoint of the anthropologist or of the neutral commentator on the customs of society.[7] The existence of predominant usage is necessary in any culture in which language is to be a simple and economical instrument of communication. The acceptance of these conventions as standards of usage is a way of maintaining uniformity. A standard of usage, then, is a way in which linguistic conventions can be and often are applied. They are conventions taken evaluatively.

The concept of a rule has recently been invoked in linguistic theory to explain how we are able to interpret an infinite or indefinite number of sentences in a language on the basis of our observation of only a finite number. Thus Fodor and Katz have written,

> Since a fluent speaker is able to use and understand any sentence drawn from the *infinite* set of sentences of his language, and since, at any time, he has only encountered a *finite* set of sentences, it follows that the speaker's knowledge of his language takes the form of rules which project the finite set of sentences he has fortuitously encountered to the infinite set of sentences of the language.[8]

7. H. L. A. Hart calls the second and third interpretations the internal and external points of view with respect to rules. See *The Concept of Law* (Oxford: Clarendon Press, 1961), pp. 86-87.

8. Fodor and Katz, *The Structure of Language*, p. 482. In a similar vein, Noam Chomsky has written: "Knowledge of a language involves the implicit ability to understand indefinitely many sentences. Hence, a generative grammar must be a system of rules that can iterate to generate an indefinitely large number of structures" (*Aspects of the*

Their claim here is too strong. The conclusion "The speaker's knowledge of his language takes the form of rules. . . ." does not strictly follow from the fact of his understanding an infinite set of sentences on the basis of his encounter with a finite set. It is logically possible that an omnipotent and omniscient demon, by ad hoc interventions, causes speakers to use and understand any one of the infinite number of sentences they might encounter. A more modest formulation is that the conclusion represents the best explanation of the speaker's competence.

The question here is what is meant by introducing the concept of a rule. There is no doubt that the speaker's competence is grounded upon repeatable features of the members of the finite set of sentences he encounters, and that these features are projected and used to interpret sentences not previously encountered. But why should these features be called rules? Fodor and Katz themselves tend to shift between the language of rules and that of regularities.

> A grammar is a system of statements employing theoretical concepts to formulate regularities in the phenomena under study. . . . The rules of grammar, thus being law-like statements, operate under the same sorts of empirical constraints as do law-like statements in other sciences. . . . The rules of grammar make predictions. . . . A grammar provides explanations of phenomena.[9]

Theory of Syntax [Cambridge, Mass.: MIT Press, 1965], pp. 15-16). The system of rules that the speaker is supposed to know need not be in his consciousness. "This is not to say that he is aware of the rules of the grammar or even that he can become aware of them, or that statements about his intuitive knowledge of the language are necessarily accurate. Any interesting generative grammar will be dealing, for the most part, with mental processes that are far beyond the level of actual or potential consciousness" (p. 18).

9. Fodor and Katz, *The Structure of Language*, pp. 153-54.

One explanation of the temptation to use the language of
rules is that the repeatable features abstracted by the language learner are not simple qualities, but rather structural
features of sentences and complex relations among sentences.

In logic it is customary to define the notion of a grammatical sentence or of a well-formed formula (*wff*) by means
of a recursive definition. There is reason to think that the
grammatical "rules" of a natural language that define what
it is to be a sentence in the language are analogous to recursive definitions. So let us examine briefly a familiar
definition, using a version of the propositional calculus in
which the *wff*s are built up from sentence letters "*P*," "*Q*,"
"*R*," and so on, and the logical constant for negation is
represented by "∼" and for conjunction is represented by
"&." The definition goes as follows:

> (1) Every sentence letter is a *wff*.
> (2) If *P* is a *wff*, then ∼ (*P*) is a *wff*.
> (3) If *P* is a *wff* and *Q* is a *wff* then (*P*)
>   & (*Q*) is a *wff*.
> (4) No expression is a *wff* unless its being
>   so follows from (1), (2), and (3).

Using this definition we can establish that "∼((*Q*) & (*R*))"
is a *wff*. By (1) we know that "*Q*" and "*R*" are *wff*s; by
(3) we know that "(*Q*) & (*R*) is a *wff*; and finally by (2)
we learn that "∼((*Q*) & (*R*))" is a *wff*. Its being a *wff* is a
feature that it possesses in virtue of its being built up in
the way it is out of its constituents. Let us call such a feature a *generative-structural attribute*. Our knowledge that
some given expression is a *wff* is derived from its generative-structural attributes, and these can be determined
by applying the recursive definition to the expression.

Whether or not the recursive definition is a rule depends

upon what is meant by "rule" and upon the standpoint
from which the language is being regarded. If we are teach-
ing someone the propositional calculus and want him to get
the grammar straight, then the definition might function as
a standard of correct usage; we might use the definition as
a means of evaluating the pupil's answers to questions about
what is and what is not a *wff*. In other circumstances we
might simply be recording systems of the propositional
calculus that others have used. This would be the external
standpoint, in which the definition functions not as our
standard of correct usage but as our record of the standard
of others. Consider now the circumstance in which we present to someone one expression after another and tell him
which one is a *wff* and which not; his task is to acquire the
ability to identify *wff*s on his own. He might be able to do
this without being able to formulate the definition. He
might be given the further task of stating in general terms
what makes an expression a *wff*. One way of doing so
would be to come up with the definition. In this case the
definition would function as a description of the generative-
structural attributes of expressions in virtue of which they
are called *wff*s. Or the definition could function as a description of the behavior of logicians to explain why they
call certain expressions *wff*s. I conclude that whether or
not the definition is a rule does not depend upon any of
its intrinsic features but upon how it is being used in a given
context. But however it is being used, there is a clear sense
in which it formulates a linguistic convention. It is not always appropriate, then, to introduce the language of rules
whenever conventions are under discussion. What a speaker
knows when he is able to interpret a sentence that he has
never previously encountered is, in part, its generative-
structural attributes. And these attributes are conventional
indicators of sentencehood. Whether what he knows is also

a rule depends upon the particular circumstances in which he is using his knowledge.

Conventions and Purposes

The discussion of rules has not carried us any further in understanding what a convention is. We are still left with the problem of distinguishing between conventional and natural regularities. In this section I shall list several features that I think account for this difference in a large class of cases. Before doing this, however, it must be understood that such a list is not intended as a logical analysis of a preexisting concept of convention. This concept of convention is, basically, a technical notion applied in various ways in the history of philosophy; it has been used to mark a felt distinction between various kinds of phenomena such as word-meanings and greetings, on the one hand, and the fact that smoke causes fire and that cold causes ice, on the other. The discussion that follows is an attempt to note some of the things that constitute the distinction rather than to analyze a well-defined preexisting concept.

Let x and y be events such that when x occurs in the appropriate circumstances, then y usually, often, or regularly occurs. One of the factors that can make the co-occurrence of x and y conventional is that x is a human action that is done for the purpose of bringing about y. Let us call this the *teleological* aspect of convention. That shaking hands is a conventional way of greeting is constituted in part by the fact that people shake hands for the purpose of greeting one another. That pointing in a certain direction is a conventional sign of signaling turns is in part constituted by the fact that people point in that way for the purpose of signaling turns. That the word "red" means a certain color by convention is in part constituted by the fact that people say and write the word with the purpose of referring to that color.

On the other hand, that smoke co-occurs with fire is not dependent on the supposition that fire burns in order to yield smoke—such a supposition is plainly false.[10] The teleological aspect explains the fact that conventions are supposed to be dependent for their very existence upon the existence of persons and their practices and institutions. Without persons who are capable of adopting means to achieve their ends in a regular way, there would be no conventions.

However, a connection between x and y can be teleological without being conventional. People use hammers to push nails into wood; they use automobiles to go from one place to another. Yet these results do not follow upon their causes by convention. A further feature that is necessary for a relationship between two events to be conventional is that the connection be *arbitrary*. It is not arbitrary that a hammer is a good way of pushing nails into wood or that an automobile is a good way of going from one place to another; hammers and automobiles are peculiarly fitted by their physical structure to serve these ends. But shaking hands is not peculiarly fitted for greeting; there are many other ways by which greeting could be accomplished that are just as practical. The word "red" is not especially suited to refer to red; another word would have done just as well. The notion of an arbitrary connection means that, because x is not peculiarly fitted by its structure or makeup for achieving y, there are alternatives that could just as well be used to accomplish the same end.

To establish conventionality, a third condition is required as well. Suppose a group of persons did x for the sake of y,

10. Of course persons may light fires for the purpose of causing smoke. But that smoke occurs is not constituted by the fact that fires are sometimes lit for this purpose.

but the fact that each one did it was a coincidence; they did not do it knowing or expecting that the others would do it. In that case, although their behavior would be in conformity with a regularity, we could not say that it was being guided by one, and thus we could not say that they were following a convention. The regularity would be accidental, but it is necessary to a convention that it not be accidental, that persons follow it because they expect others to do so as well.

Let us summarize the conditions for the existence of a convention in the following rough definition:

The co-occurrence of x and y is a conventional regularity among a group of persons provided:

(1) the members of the group do x for the purpose of y

(2) the connection between x and y is arbitrary

(3) the members of the group expect one another to do x for the sake of y, and this is a reason why they do x for the sake of y.

5 Meaning

Speaker's Meaning and Performatives

Given, then, that the notion of purpose is essential to that of convention, how shall we assess Austin's claim that illocutionary acts are conventional? Before directly confronting this question, we must clear up certain confusions that could interfere with an adequate answer to it. Earlier I argued that in one sense of use, the meaning of a sentence can be identified with that sentence's use.[1] But it is clearly necessary to distinguish between the use of a sentence and what a speaker means by it on a given occasion. What the speaker means may coincide with its use in whole or in part, or his meaning may fail to coincide with its use at all. The sentence "That is red" has as a use the capacity to state that some object in the vicinity is of red color, and it does not have as a use the capacity to state of some object that it is of yellow color. If a speaker mistakenly believes that "red" means yellow, he might utter, "That is red," meaning that that is yellow. In that case what the speaker means fails to coincide with what the sentence means. Clearly the existence of successful communication and mutual understanding depend upon the speaker's meaning coinciding with sentence-meaning in most cases just because sentence-meaning is the primary evidence we have for determining what a speaker means.

When a speaker is asked what he meant when he uttered a given sentence, there is a certain form—a fully explicit statement of speaker's meaning—that his answer can always

1. See chapter 2.

take; examples are: "I meant to state that two plus three equals five"; "I meant to ask how the weather is"; "I meant to promise to return the book." The general schema is "I meant to *a*," where the variable "*a*" takes performative acts as its values. In a fully explicit statement of speaker's meaning, the word "meant" (or "mean") can be replaced by "intended" (or "intend") or, with some verbal shift, by "purpose," as in "My purpose was to state that two plus three equals five." Speaker's meaning is nothing but the intention or purpose to do some performative act.[2]

Occasionally, however, persons fail to achieve what they intend, either through an error on their part or through some interfering factor in the context of action. In the case of linguistic actions it is not always easy to know how to classify cases of failure. Consider the following case: S says to L, "I will return the book soon," meaning his utterance as a promise; L, however, fails to hear S because his attention is diverted; S does not realize this and believes himself to be bound by a promise. Was the promise really made? Shall we say that S really did promise L although L failed to realize it, or shall we say that S tried but failed to make a promise? Here is another case: S says to L, "Close the window," intending this as an order; L replies (correctly, let us suppose), "You have no authority to order me about; I shall not close the window." Shall we say that S tried to order L but failed, or shall we say that S really did order L, but L is under no obligation to obey?

There is no difficulty in these cases in describing the facts; the problem lies in determining whether the facts justify asserting that the speaker did succeed in doing some peform-

2. The term "mean" is often interchangeable with "intend" even in nonlinguistic cases as in "I intend (mean) to take a walk on the beach."

ative act or merely that he meant to achieve his intention
but failed. Because these are borderline cases, it does not
matter much what we say, and I shall refrain from verbal
legislation. I shall just leave such borderline cases as another
category; there is no need to accommodate them among the
clear successes or clear failures.

The cases just considered lean toward failure because of
some contextual feature. But the difficulty may also be in
the form of words actually used, as in these cases: (1) S intends to state that elephants have big ears; but thinking
that "rabbit" means elephant, he says, "Rabbits have
big ears." (2) S intends to state that elephants have big
ears; he knows the correct meaning of "elephant" and "rabbit" and intends to say, "Elephants have big ears," but he
absentmindedly says, "Rabbits have big ears." What statement did S actually make in these cases? He intended to
state that elephants have big ears, but in each case he used
a sentence whose meaning is that rabbits have big ears. Is
the statement he made the one he intended to make, the
one given by his fully explicit statement of speaker's meaning, or the one that he would normally be understood to
have made on the basis of the sentence-meaning? Doubts
as to how to answer this question cannot be reduced by in-
vestigating S's own responses to his error, since these can be
subjected to the same questions. Upon realizing that he used
the incorrect word, S might avow, "I meant to say that
elephants have big ears." This avowal, however, can be subjected to multiple interpretations. S might mean that in making the statement that elephants have big ears, he should have
used the sentence "Elephants have big ears." Or alternatively,
he might mean that he had intended to state that elephants
have big ears rather than to state, as he did, that rabbits
have big ears.

Because speaker's meaning and sentence-meaning do coincide in the vast majority of cases, our concepts of various performative actions do not tell us and do not need to tell us how they should be applied in those cases where there is a lack of coincidence. As long as the facts of the case are clear, that is, as long as we can specify the speaker's meaning and the sentence-meaning and take note of the points where they do and do not coincide, there is no philosophical reason to accommodate borderline cases to one concept or another. Of course, there may be practical reasons to search for an accommodation; if a person's slip of the tongue should affect the terms of a legally binding agreement, those whose task it is to settle legal disputes must find a general principle to resolve the indeterminacy at hand. Moreover, there are some cases in which reference to the speaker's meaning conclusively resolves the indeterminacy; for example, in cases of ambiguity—where a sentence is susceptible of more than one interpretation, as in "The shooting of the hunters was quite distressing"—what the speaker intended settles the question as to which interpretation is applicable on a particular occasion. But in ambiguity we do not have a discrepancy between speaker's meaning and sentence-meaning; rather, we are in doubt as to which sentence-meaning is the applicable one.

Putting to one side the borderline cases, we can say that whenever a person carries out a performative action, there is a fully explicit statement he could make of his meaning or intention that would tell us which act he performed. Thus the notion of purpose does seem to be directly involved with the idea of a nonproblematic linguistic action.

The Constitution of Performatives

To say that when a linguistic action is performed, there exists in the speaker the aim of performing just that action is not to demonstrate that intentions or purposes are in any sense constitutive of performatives; after all, the aims have been described by reference to performatives and are not conceptually prior to them. If, however, it can be shown that fully explicit statements of speaker's meaning can be explained by reference to certain other aims of the speaker, then it would be demonstrated that performatives are constituted from these aims.

In a well-known article H. P. Grice has developed a theory of meaning that shows promise of being adaptable to a theory of linguistic actions even though he has not formulated it in just these terms.[3] He distinguishes initially between two kinds of meaning—natural and nonnatural—which are intended to correspond to the traditional distinction between the natural and conventional meaning of signs. Nonnatural meaning is explicated by reference to the intentions of speakers: what a speaker means is what he intends to bring about by his utterance; what his utterance means is what persons usually intend to bring about by that utterance. He sums up his view in the following generalizations:

(1) "A meant something by x" is (roughly) equivalent to "A intended the utterance of x to produce some effect in an audience by means of the recognition of this intention" . . . .

(2) "x meant something" is (roughly) equivalent to "Somebody meant something by x" . . . .

(3) "x means$_{NN}$(timeless) that so-and-so" might as a first shot be equated with some statement or disjunction of statements about what "people" (vague) intend (with qualifications about "recognition") to effect by x.[4]

3. H. P. Grice, "Meaning," *The Philosophical Review* 66 (July 1957): 377-88.
4. Ibid., p. 385.

Grice does not restrict the values of the variable x to linguistic entities, because things other than words can have nonnatural meaning. But when the values are linguistic entities, it is clear from the way the definitions are formulated that they are full sentences and not individual words. Because of this, (3) is inadequate, since it presupposes that in order for a sentence to have meaning, there must be standard intentions for its use and therefore, contrary to fact, it must have been used on previous occasions. In addition, (2) does not conform to the conclusions of our previous discussion. Recall the example of someone meaning to state that elephants have big ears but actually saying, "Rabbits have big ears." Although it is true that the speaker meant something by this sentence, that is, he intended to make a certain statement, it does not follow that what the sentence meant on that occasion is that elephants have big ears. In fact, we have no use at all for the notion of a sentence's having a certain meaning on an occasion of its being spoken. If a sentence has several interpretations, then we might wish to know under which interpretation it was being spoken on a given occasion, but that interpretation is fixed by the G-S structure of the sentence and is not determined by speaker's meaning. There is no useful notion of sentence-meaning in which what a sentence means is strictly deducible from what the speaker means on a given occasion.[5]

5. In a later article ("Utterer's Meaning and Intentions," *The Philosophical Review* 78 [April 1969] : 147-77) Grice introduces several distinctions relevant to this point. What he there calls the timeless meaning of a sentence corresponds to the various uses a sentence has. What he calls the applied timeless meaning corresponds to the interpretation under which a sentence is spoken on a given occasion. The type of meaning he defines in (2) is there described by him as the occasion-meaning. My point can be summarized in his terms by saying that there is no such thing as the occasion-meaning of a sentence.

For our purposes, definition (1) is most important. When A speaks a sentence T, then his meaning something by T is what I have called speaker's meaning. In the fully explicit statement of speaker's meaning, it becomes clear that what is meant is the performance of some performative action. Because in the fully explicit statement, "intends" can be substituted for "means," I can agree with Grice that speaker's meaning is a certain kind of intention. Although his analysis does not explicitly mention performatives at all, it provides for them by implication by supposing that the different kinds of sentences that are typically used to perform different kinds of performatives—indicatives for statements, imperatives for commands, interrogatives for questions—are associated with intentions to produce different types of effects upon the audience. Earlier I took note of Austin's distinction between illocutionary and perlocutionary acts, the latter being effects of the former. Grice's approach, with the interpretations of it I have proposed, consists in explaining linguistic actions as speech expressed with the intention of bringing about certain perlocutionary results. This theory implies that the notions of illocutionary and perlocutionary acts are not logically independent of each other. In developing this approach in detail, I shall use some of Grice's discussion wherever it is helpful, but in general I will pursue an independent line.

Statements and Purposes

Consider this example: there is a standard context of communication between two persons, S and L; L asks S where the cat is, and S responds by uttering the sentence "The cat is on the mat." What plausible construction can we place on S's purposes in uttering that sentence other than the obvious one that he intended to state that the cat is on the mat? Let us suppose that the cat really is on the mat and that S knows this. One of S's aims, then, is to bring about a certain state of belief in L. This cannot be the end of the story, however, because the fact that S used words to bring about this belief means that he also aimed at creating this belief in a certain way. The belief could have been created in alternate ways—it is theoretically possible to operate on L's brain to cause him to believe that the cat is on the mat, but such an operation would not be a statement. In this case L is supposed to believe that the cat is on the mat because he believes that S believes it. In making the statement, S is communicating his own belief to L and wants L to accept it because S accepts it.

In reviewing the example, we can see that with respect to S's aims, there are, so far, two beliefs of primary importance:

(1) The cat is on the mat.
(2) S believes that the cat is on the mat.

S's first aim is to cause L to accept (1). His second aim is to cause L to accept (2). And his third aim is that L's belief in (2) be a reason for his belief in (1). There is also one further aim that should be mentioned. In standard contexts of communication, the aims of the speaker are open and above board; he wants his auditors to believe that his aim in speaking is to communicate information to them and to give them reasons for accepting this information. So S's fourth aim is to cause L to believe that S intends him to accept (1) on the basis of (2). S's intentions can be summed up in the following schema:

(A) In speaking the sentence T, S intends to bring it
    about that:
    (a) L believes that p,
    (b) L believes that S believes that p,
    (c) L has as a reason for his believing that p his belief that S believes that p.

  (d) L believes that S intends him to believe that
      p on the basis that S believes p.

Schema (A) does represent a plausible description of some of
the aims of a speaker in a standard statement-making situation. Shall we also say that (A) provides an adequate analysis of what it means to say that S means to state that p?
Suppose it does. Then it is obvious that if S's speech occurs
without any hitches, then (A) also tells us what it means for
S to state that p. Therefore, (A) would be an essential constituent of a general theory of performative actions.

  Can anything be said in favor of (A) as an analysis of the
notion of making a statement? Before considering objections to this claim, there are two arguments in its favor that
I would like to mention. Whether these arguments are ulti-
mately successful depends upon how well this analysis of
statement-making stands up to criticism. The first argument
(A_1) is simply that whatever faults in detail there might be
with the analysis as so far presented, there is no alternative
to an analysis of this kind. We do know that statements express and communicate what people believe; belief seems
to be the state of mind most directly correlated with statements. When a person makes a statement, what else can
enter into an explanation of what he does than the sentence
he uttered and the aims with which he uttered it? What can
it be to mean to make a statement if not to aim at producing certain beliefs in the auditors? To reject this analysis is
to make the notion of statement-making mysterious. Later
we shall examine a crucial reply to this argument, which
will lead us to modify the analysis.

The Paradox of Belief

  One who would reject an analysis of this type may do so
on the grounds that the connections between making a
statement and having the intention to produce certain be-

liefs is contingent—that there is no logical or conceptual connection between these notions. Argument (A$_2$) tries to defend schema (A) against this objection by showing that there is a form of conceptual connection. Suppose that S says to L,

(1) The cat is on the mat, and I do not believe it.

There is no doubt that (1) or, for that matter, anything of the form "p and I do not believe that p" is an odd thing to say. Now what makes it odd cannot be that (1) is necessarily false, for it can possibly be true. For example, suppose S does not believe that the cat is on the mat but his belief is mistaken; then, what (1) says is true. We therefore need another explanation of why (1) seems peculiar. What is odd about (1) is not what it says, but that it should be said by S; the oddness of (1) is derived from the oddness of

(2) S states that the cat is on the mat and that he does not believe that the cat is on the mat.

But what is odd about (2)? It cannot be that (2) is necessarily false, for it may very well be true. The oddness of (2) can be explained plausibly if we accept the following general principle:

(3) If S states to L that p, then S intends to bring it about that L believes that S believes that p.

This principle together with (2) implies

(4) S intends to bring it about that L believes that S believes that the cat is on the mat.

Thus if S should utter (1), then one of the things he wants to get L to believe (namely, that he believes the cat is on the mat) explicitly contradicts one of the things that he explicitly says to L (namely, that he does not believe it). Therefore his statement, though not logically inconsistent, is logically incoherent; its incoherence lies in the fact that L cannot determine what S really does believe. What makes this incoherence a matter of logic is that it is due to the logical inconsistency between the statement made and the belief intended.

We can provide a slightly different explanation if, in addition to (3), we can also accept as a principle,

> (5) If S states to L that p, then S intends to bring it about that L believes p.

Now (3), (5), and (2) jointly imply

> (6) S intends to bring it about that L believes that S believes and does not believe that the cat is on the mat.

According to this explanation, (2) is odd because it implies that S intends L to believe an explicit contradiction. And if we accept the further assumption that it is logically impossible for anyone to believe an explicit contradiction, then what S intends is logically impossible of fulfillment.

Thus (3) by itself and (3) together with (5) provide plausible explanations for the oddness of (1) and show, what has long been felt, that the oddness stems from the logical structure of (1). To the extent to which these explanations are superior to alternatives, they tend to confirm both (3) and (5) and thus a portion of the analysis of the schema of statement making, namely (A(a) and (b)).

A Fundamental Objection

Earlier I argued that sentence-meaning could plausibly be identified with sentence-use where a use of a sentence was defined as the capacity of one of its interpretations to be used to perform some performative actions and not others *as determined by the G-S structure of the sentence.* The italicized clause implies that it is the sentence's G-S structure and not the aims with which it is spoken that determine or at least circumscribe the act that is performed. When someone says, "The cat is on the mat," the statement he makes can be directly determined by interpreting the sentence in the light of knowledge of the English language; there is no need to make inferences to the speaker's intentions.

In a critique of Grice's account of meaning, Paul Ziff presents several examples that illustrate this point.[6] I shall adapt one of them to my formulation of the account. Suppose S utters, "The cat is on the mat" on three occasions on the same day: on the first occasion he speaks it to himself, on the second to L, and on the third he speaks it while delirious with fever. On the first and third occasions, it is implausible to ascribe to S any of the aims listed in schema (A), and yet one can say that on all three occasions he has made the same statement. Since, the objection goes, the stipulated aims can vary or even be absent, clearly they have nothing to do with what is being said.

Earlier, in discussing certain objections to psychologism, I stressed the fact of the objectivity of meaning by pointing out that speakers select the words and sentences they utter in the light of their antecedently determinate meaning. If what they said was a function of their contemporary intentions, communication would be impossible. It is because meanings are objective and common and not a function of present psychological states that speakers can understand one another.

6. Paul Ziff, "On H. P. Grice's Account of Meaning," *Analysis* 28 (October 1967): 1-8.

Although this objection certainly rings true, it appears to conflict with another point I established earlier. That a given string of words has a particular G-S structure in virtue of which it means one thing rather than another was shown to be a matter of convention. My analysis of the notion of convention makes essential use of the notion of intention or purpose. How, then, can this be reconciled with the objection?

If we scrutinize the sentence "The cat is on the mat," we shall notice that there are several conventions relevant to determining its G-S structure. There are, first of all, the conventions that determine the meanings of the individual words that make up the sentence—*lexical conventions.* There are also the *syntactic conventions* that determine how the words combine with each other to form meaningful groupings—how "the" combines with "cat" and "mat," how "on" combines with "the mat," how "the cat" combines with "is" and "on the mat." The sentence as a whole is of the form "x is Ry" where "x" and "y" represent singular terms and "R" a preposition. Other sentences of that form are "The pen is above the table"; "The man is over the hill"; "Socrates is next to Alcibiades." Sentences of the form "x is Ry" are characteristically used to make statements, just as sentences with the copula positioned differently, as in "Is xRy," are characteristically used to ask questions. That these two forms are related to these two types of performative action is a matter of convention. According to my analysis of the notion of convention, it follows that these forms acquire their conventional significance as a result of people using them for the purpose of making statements on the one hand and asking questions on the other. If people changed their habits and used the form "Is xRy" for statements and "x is Ry" for questions, the conventions would change, and the forms would acquire a new conventional significance.

It is important to realize that there is no convention that determines the meaning of "The cat is on the mat" or of any other sentence as a whole. Although words and syntactic forms are regulated by conventions, sentences are not. So, in a sense, that a given sentence is used to do a certain performative action is not itself a matter of convention. Sentence-meaning or sentence-use is not conventional in the same way that word-meaning is. But it does not follow that sentence-meaning is natural. The truth of the matter is that sentence-meaning is a result of the sum total of lexical and syntactical conventions applicable to the sentence. If a person utters "The cat is on the mat" in accordance with the usual conventions, then he has made the statement that the cat is on the mat, no matter what intentions accompanied his speech.[7] For this reason the aims listed in schema (A), while they may accompany the making of many or most statements, cannot be constitutive of what it means to make a particular statement. Therefore, I must agree with the fundamental objection. In addition, there is no conflict between that objection and the fact that a given sentence has the meaning it does as a matter of convention—the meaning is a matter of convention, not in the sense that there is such a convention, but rather that it is the result of conventions.

A Reconsideration

The validity of this objection means that Grice's theory in the form I have given it must be discarded. And the reason we have provided for rejecting it explains the apparent independence of speech acts from psychological states that the critics of psychologism have long pointed out. On the

7. The qualifications and exceptions discussed in chapter 5 should be kept in mind.

other hand, there is nothing in the fundamental objection
which requires that my theory of the nature of convention
must be given up as well. This theory asserts that the aims
or intentions of speakers are essential for the existence of
those linguistic conventions that apply to the constituents
and forms of sentences. That "*x* is *Ry*" can be interpreted
as being the form of a statement and "Is *xRy*" as being the
form of a question are matters of convention. But what,
then, is the conventional regularity in virtue which "*x* is
Ry" is a statement-form? One might reply that the regularity is between the occurrence of sentences of the form
"*x* is *Ry*" and the occurrence of the statements they are
used to make. But while this answer would be true, it would
be unilluminating because what needs to be explained is the
general notion of making a statement.

It seems to me that the only plausible answer to the question is this: Certain forms are of the statement-making
variety because they are most often used with the aim of
communicating information—that is, of conveying what
the speaker thinks and of causing the auditor either to
think what the speaker thinks or at least to accept that the
speaker thinks it. Other forms are of the type used to give
orders because they are most often used with the aim of
letting the hearer know what the speaker wants him to do,
and still other forms are of the question-making variety
because they are generally used with the aim of acquiring
information, that is, of eliciting a statement from the hearer.
In general, if we mention a particular performative action,
we can determine by reflection the aims that characteristically accompany actions of that type. The forms specific to
that action acquire their meaning through their being means
to the attainment of those aims.[8]

8. There need not be forms specific to a performative action. An

The existence of a conventional regularity is compatible with the existence of an indefinite number of deviations from it. If there are sufficient deviations, the convention will cease to exist. But unanimity of practice is certainly not essential to maintain its existence. It is, therefore, possible to engage in speech acts which, according to the conventions, are of a certain type without all or any of the aims characteristic of that type occurring. That is why it is possible to make a statement in a delirium or in a soliloquy even though it is not possible for all or even most statements to occur this way. The reason why schema (A) fails as an analysis of what it means to make a statement is that the occurrence of the specified aims are not necessary for the making of a particular statement, even though the occurrence of these aims in a wide though indefinite number of contexts is necessary for the form of the sentence to be of the statement-making variety.

But what about the two arguments I earlier advanced in favor of Grice's analysis. The first argument (A_1—see p. 66) was basically that there seemed to be no alternative. And we can still accept this argument, merely modifying it to apply not to individual occurrences of speech acts but rather to general types. The second argument (A_2—see pp. 66-68) was based upon the paradox of belief. It involved two basic principles—(3) and (5)—relating statements to intentions to cause certain beliefs. My analysis of why speaking (1) is odd can still remain as there provided. The two basic principles, however, must be interpreted, not as stating logically necessary conditions for the making of statements, but as assert-

---

insult is a species of statement, for example, and the forms specific to it are of the statement-making sort; what makes a statement an insult is the type of belief communicated and the intention to injure in communicating it.

ing generalizations holding often enough to establish the conventions for the making of statements.

The approach here sketched for the analysis of performative actions does vindicate psychologism. Although the occurrence of an individual performative does not provide a logical guarantee of the occurrence of any associated psychological state, nevertheless, there are characteristic aims and intentions that are necessary for the existence of the conventions that make performatives possible.

Word-Meaning

Word-meaning is no less conventional than sentence-meaning. While the latter is a result of lexical and syntactic conventions, the meanings of words and smaller particles are directly determined by conventions. How shall these conventions be characterized and understood?

The fundamental assumption behind the approach delineated in this volume is that as far as meaning is concerned, the basic reality consists of linguistic actions. These are the data on the basis of which language learners acquire their ability to interpret the speech of others and to speak themselves.[9] To understand the meanings of an individual word it is necessary to grasp the convention under which it is used. These lexical conventions, when they are recorded in words and used, as in dictionaries, to explain the meanings of words, are called definitions. Let us examine some of the forms that definitions can take in order to gain some insight into the nature of lexical conventions. First consider:

9. I am not taking sides on the current dispute over the issue of innate linguistic capacities. This is an empirical question in the broadest sense that can be resolved, if at all, only by detailed research into the mechanisms of learning. But all parties to the dispute agree that these mechanisms, whatever their internal complexity, are applied to linguistic actions as the basic data.

(1) "Crimson" means a shade of deep red color inclining toward purple.

A possible way of interpreting (1) is to think of the word "means" as representing a relation between the word "crimson" and the color it signifies. Taking the notion of relation broadly and loosely, there is no objection to this interpretation. There is, however, a technical notion of relation according to which whenever an entity x bears a relation to an entity y, both x and y exist. And yet the object of the verb "means" does not always name something that exists, for example, consider the meaning of "centaur." Even waiving this objection, it is not always true that the object of "means" is a substantive capable of naming an entity. Witness:

(2) "le" (in French) means the.

It is plausible to interpret (2) as simply being an abbreviation for

(3) The word "le" has a use in French similar to the use "the" has in English.

This interpretation may seem to vindicate Wittgenstein's dictum that meaning is use. But it is less plausible when applied to (1). Is it possible to think of (1) as an abbreviated statement of use?

Why should a speaker of English use the word "crimson"? Let us consider some examples. "The color of that chair is crimson": here "crimson" occurs as a substantive and is used to classify a certain shade of color, to say what color it is. "Crimson is the color you want for your walls": here "crimson" again is used as a substantive to single out or identify a particular color as the one that is wanted. "The walls are crimson"; "The crimson walls are ugly": here "crimson," occurring as an adjective, first as a predicate and second as a modifier, is used to communicate what quality a certain object has. The word thus has the multiple functions of classification, identification, and qualification. Our ability to distinguish among these functions in the examples depends upon a number of factors. For instance, in two cases "crimson" follows a form of the verb "to be"; yet in the first case it is a substantive and in the second an adjective. The way we make the distinction is this: In "The color of that chair is crimson" it is implausible to interpret "is" as introducing a qualification, for colors are qualities and do not themselves have colors as qualities. It would be a category mistake to interpret "is" as representing qualification.[10] But in "The walls are crimson" we know that "are" cannot introduce a classification because walls, though they have colors as qualities, are not themselves shades of colors.

The answer to the question "Why should a speaker of English want to use the word 'crimson'?" is this: there are certain activities he may wish to perform such as singling out a color or classifying one or qualifying an object with one. What is common to these various activities is the particular color—crimson—the speaker has in mind. Formulation (1) is thus justified as a statement of the feature common to the various functions of the word. A complete and adequate definition would list, along with this common feature, the basic types of activities or uses of the word. In fact, however, it is unnecessary for dictionaries to give complete and adequate definitions, since one who speaks English or a language similar to it already knows the various uses of words and interprets (1) accordingly. Usually a dictionary

10. Since our ability to identify correct and incorrect category relations is used here as a basis for interpreting speech, this is evidence that such relations are not themselves derived from language but are nonlinguistic facts "in the world."

will provide a definition richer in information than (1), which goes part of the way toward specifying various uses. Consider this extract from the entry for "red" from *The Shorter Oxford English Dictionary:*

> [4] **Red.** A. *adj* Having, or characterized by the colour which appears at the lower or least refracted end of the visible spectrum, and is familiar as that of blood, fire, the poppy, the rose, and ripe fruits. . . . B. *sb*. Red colour; redness. Often with defining terms prefixed, as *alizarin, cherry,* etc.

We understand the definition for "red" as an adjective in this way: its most typical adjectival occurrence is in the predicate position as in "The walls are red"; someone who speaks this sentence is asserting that the walls have the color red or are characterized by that color. The definition explains this typical occurrence. Clearly it does not explain its occurrence in "The walls are not red," for in this we are not characterizing the walls by that color, even though it occurs here as an adjective as well. But it is taken for granted that one who grasps the use explained and who has mastered English can gather on his own how the word functions in other contexts. The definition for "red" as a substantive or noun simply provides other nouns or noun phrases that name the same color— "red color" and "redness"; by describing it as a substantive the entry alludes to certain other functions of the word such as identifying or classifying a color. One who has mastered English and who knows what a substantive is, that is, in what positions it can occur in speech, can use the entry to interpret such sentences as "Red is the color of the walls," "The color of the candle is not red," and so on.

When we talk about the meaning of a word, what we are really discussing are its various typical uses by speakers of the language. Definitions or explanations of the meaning are usually succinct or abbreviated formulations of the most central use or uses from which the less central ones can be gathered by one who has mastered the language. Occasionally, a definition will communicate the meaning merely by listing another word having the same or similar uses presumably known to the reader. The conventional regularities in virtue of which words have the meaning they do consists in precisely these uses. But this needs further explanation.

Word-Use: Subordinate Linguistic Actions

Meaning is use, as Wittgenstein suggested. But what does this amount to? In the previous section three word-uses were mentioned—identification, classification, and qualification. Identification occurs when a person singles out or identifies something; classification when a person classifies something; and qualification when a person ascribes a quality to or qualifies something. These uses, then, are things that people do with words; they are linguistic acts. But they are not linguistic acts of the kind we have already discussed— performatives and illocutionary acts. For in these the minimal linguistic unit is the sentence. Performative actions are things we do with sentences (even if they contain only one word) and passages consisting of sentences. The linguistic actions here mentioned are those we do with the words in a sentence as a means of producing a performative action. They are subordinate linguistic actions.

Let us reflect upon a simple example. S says, "The wall is crimson." In so doing, he has accomplished the performative action of stating that the wall is crimson. In making this statement he has also done the following: first, he has singled out or identified a particular object—the wall—to say something about; this is the use of "the wall." Second, he has ascribed a quality to the object singled out or identified; the word "crimson" here tells which quality is being ascribed; the phrase "is crimson" indicates that as a whole what is going on is qualification rather than questioning a qualification (as in "Is the wall crimson?") or denying a qualification (as in "The wall is not crimson"). In using the phrase "the wall" to single out an object for qualification, the speaker has accomplished his aim by using "wall" to tell what sort of object is being singled out—classification, and "the" to indicate that one and only one particular instance of this sort—the one pointed at or previously identified—is meant. In describing these subordinate linguistic actions, we have invariably mentioned the aims of the speaker: identification is using a word or phrase in order to single out a particular object; qualification is using a word or phrase with the intention of ascribing a quality to an object, and so forth. The conventions that determine the meanings of words consist of words being used for these purposes, and changes in these conventions result in alteration of meaning. Definitions are merely abbreviated records of the aims of speakers.

A person who has mastered the language and knows the meanings of many of its words knows the conventions in accordance with which these words are used. But he does not know them as a spectator who has noticed and recorded the habits of other speakers. Rather, he has been trained to act in accordance with these conventions; such training causes his behavior and intentions to match that of others. A person is able to state explicitly the standard meaning of a word because, upon reflecting upon the circumstances under which he would employ the word, he can state his characteristic aims in using it, and since his aims approximate those of others, his statement can be generalized to the rest of the speech community.

Part II

Philosophical Implications and Applications

6   Nature and Convention

Intentional Meaning

The explanation of the nature of meaning developed in Part
I agrees with the spirit of Hobbes's dictum that "the general
use of speech, is to transfer our mental discourse, into verbal;
or the train of our thoughts, into a train of words." Earlier
I reconstructed Hobbes's argument in favor of this dictum
as asserting that words acquire their conventional meaning
through association with thoughts whose meaning is not determined by conventions. In terms of my approach, this argument says that words acquire their conventional meaning as
a result of their being selected by language users to achieve
their aims in communication. What Hobbes calls "thoughts"
I have replaced by aims or purposes or intentions. To carry
through the structure of Hobbes's argument, I also want to
claim that what a person's intentions are intentions of is not
a matter of convention. The states of affairs that make sentences of the form "A intends to . . ." true are not themselves constituted by human conventions. When such a sentence is true, it follows that the person whom it is about is
in a certain mental state—that of having an intention or a
purpose. It is characteristic of many of the things we call
mental states—thoughts, intentions, certain emotions—that
they are directed to something or are about or of something.
A thought is always a thought of this or that thing; an intention is always an intention to do this or that; a person
in the emotional state of fear is afraid of this or that. This
feature of mental states has been called intentionality. That
which the mental state is directed toward or is about has
been called its *content*. That a certain person's mental state

has a certain content is not itself a matter of convention.[1]
In point of terminology, I want to say that a mental state
means its content, but since this is not the sort of meaning
constituted by linguistic conventions, I shall mark it by
calling it *intentional meaning* or *meaning (i)* for short.
When a person, then, is thinking that the cat is on the mat,
there is a certain mental event, his thinking that the cat is
on the mat, which means (i) that the cat is on the mat.
When a person intends to take a walk, there is a certain
mental state, his intending to take a walk, which means
(i) that he will take a walk. The content that is meant (i)
is represented by full sentences. The basic schema for meaning (i) assertions is:

(1) M means (i) that T

where "M" is taken as the name of a mental state or episode
of some person and "T" is a sentence which expresses the
content. The most common way of forming a name of a
mental state is by using the content-sentence, for example,
"Jones's thought that the cat is on the mat." Such a name is
intentionally transparent. When an intentionally transparent
name is used in meaning (i) assertions, the basic schema takes
the form:

(2) A's M that T means (i) that T

where for "A" is substituted a name of a person and for
"M" the name of the appropriate type of mental state or
episode, thus "Jones's thought that the cat is on the mat

1. I do not wish to deny that, as a matter of fact, people often think
in words. This means that a factual condition of having certain thoughts
is the mastery of speech. Linguistic conventions thus may constitute
causal conditions of certain intentional states. What I am claiming is
that the notion of a convention does not enter into our concept of an
intentional state.

means (i) that the cat is on the mat" and "Jones's intention that he takes a walk means (i) that he takes a walk." Statements of form (2) are true only if the person named really is in the designated mental state. When this truth condition is satisfied, the statement is then automatically true. Form (2), however, is not the only realization of (1), because there are ways of referring to mental states without using the content-sentence as in "Socrates' final thought" or "my unfortunate intention."

The theory of Part I can thus be reformulated briefly as: conventional meaning is due to intentional meaning. The way in which the first is due to the second was spelled out in some detail in the preceding chapter. As we saw, their relation is not simple; a theory such as Grice's which asserts a direct and immediate connection between the two is not acceptable as it stands.

How shall we construe schema (2)? According to one major view in semantic theory—the theory of propositions—sentences of this form assert a relation between a person (or his mental state) and a proposition. It would follow, using the technical notion of relation, that propositions, false as well as true, exist, but we have reason to doubt this view. Therefore I shall not interpret "means (i)" as it occurs in (2) as naming a relation; it follows that the object of the sentence, the phrase "that T," shall not be interpreted as a name of an existent.

There is an alternative account that I shall adopt here.[2] Statements of form (1) and (2) ascribe an attribute to the mental state referred to. Thus "Jones's thought that the cat is on the mat means (i) that the cat is on the mat" asserts

2. Readers familiar with their writings will realize the debt the subsequent discussion owes to the writings of Gustav Bergmann and Wilfrid Sellars. See particularly Bergmann's *Logic and Reality* (Madison, Wis.: University of Wisconsin Press, 1964), Essay 1, and Sellars's *Science and Metaphysics* (London: Routledge and Kegan Paul, 1968), chap. 3.

that Jones's thought has a certain attribute, namely, the attribute of meaning (i) that the cat is on the mat. When Jones is thinking that the cat is on the mat and Smith is thinking that the elephant has big ears, they are obviously having different thoughts; there must be something about the thoughts which differs in each case. On this account, they differ in that Jones's thought has the attribute of meaning (i) that the cat is on the mat and Smith's has the different attribute of meaning (i) that the elephant has big ears. Difference in content entails a difference in *intentional attributes.*

There is also the case in which the content is the same but the mental state differs, as in "Jones believes that the cat is on the mat" and "Jones doubts that the cat is on the mat." Here the same attribute, that of meaning (i) that the cat is on the mat, qualifies mental states of different species. To specify a mental state that has intentional meaning it is sufficient to mention its species and its intentional attribute.

Conventional and Intentional Meaning

The foregoing account of intentional meaning is compatible with various alternative analyses of it and of the mental states that are characterized by it. Thus nothing was said that is incompatible either with a dispositional or occurrent analysis of belief and intention nor with certain behavioristic or Cartesian accounts of the same. The account is even compatible with the materialistic view that mental states are brain states. There are many philosophers, however, who think that materialism is incompatible with the existence of intentional attributes. One reason that is often behind this view is the assumption that no physical state could mean (i) something or have a content; I reject this assumption; one cannot exclude a priori any "stuff" from meaning (i) something. Any exclusion that is to be made must be made on empirical grounds. Although the account is neutral in these ways, there is one respect in which it is not. The claim that conventional meaning is due to intentional meaning excludes any analysis of intentional meaning using concepts specific to conventional meaning. In particular, intentional meaning cannot be analyzed in terms of linguistic activity; it cannot be, say, a form of talking to oneself, nor can it be a disposition to engage in verbal behavior. Notice that what is excluded is a certain kind of analysis. I am not excluding the possibility of conventional meaning being a causal condition of certain kinds of intentional meaning; nor is my account a theory of learning: it may be that human beings only acquire intentional states when they also acquire the ability to express them in language. Nor am I claiming that intentional meaning is epistemologically prior; in fact the reverse is often true: we usually discover what mental state a person is in and what it means (i) by grasping what he says. My point is simply the negative one that the concept of intentional meaning cannot be defined in terms of conventional meaning.[3]

There is a different approach that would account for intentional meaning in terms of conventional meaning. Consider the following passages by Wilfrid Sellars:

> [1] The counterpart attributes of conceptual episodes, by virtue of which they, in their own way, stand for their senses, are to be construed on the analogy

3. Thus I agree with the spirit, though not the details of Aristotle's view in chapter 1 of *De Interpretatione:* "Spoken words are symbols of mental experience and written words are the symbols of spoken words. Just as all men have not the same writing, so all men have not the same speech sounds, but the mental experiences, which these directly symbolize, are the same for all."

of whatever it is about linguistic episodes by virtue
of which they stand for their senses.

[2] The *metalinguistic* vocabulary in which we talk about
linguistic episodes can be analysed in terms which
do not presuppose the framework óf mental acts;
in particular, that
     ". . ." means p
is not to be analysed as
     ". . ." expresses t and t is about p
where t is a thought.[4]

I interpret (2) as denying the thesis that conventional meaning
is due to intentional meaning. And I understand (1) as com-
ing close to asserting the converse, namely that intentional
meaning is due to conventional meaning.[5]

The defense of my thesis was grounded in my analysis of
the notion of convention, which involves the idea of purpose or intention and thus of intentional meaning. A view

4. (1) is from *Science and Metaphysics,* pp. 66-67, and (2) is from
the "Chisholm-Sellars Correspondence on Intentionality," *Minnesota
Studies in the Philosophy of Science,* vol. 2 (Minneapolis: University
of Minnesota Press, 1958), p. 522. Both of these passages are rough
formulations of large-scale philosophical programs and should be interpreted accordingly.

5. It is difficult to interpret (1) because Sellars qualifies it in various
places. Thus in his correspondence with Chisholm (p. 530) he writes:
"Indeed, I have explicitly denied . . . that thoughts (and consequently
their aboutness) are to be *defined* in terms of language. I have, however, argued that the aboutness of thoughts is to be *explained* or *understood* by reference to the categories of semantical discourse about
language." Thus he would accept the thesis Chisholm ascribes to him
(p. 529): "The meaning of thoughts is to be analysed in terms of the
meaning of language, and not conversely" only if the notion of analysis is weakly interpreted. Chisholm's last letter (p. 537) discusses
the relevant notions of analysis.

that would prescind the notion of a convention from a relation to mind cannot, I think, distinguish between conventional and natural regularities. On the other hand, it is important to understand such views. There are several reasons, I think, why a philosopher may be inclined to adopt (1) and (2) or something like these.

First, he may argue that the notion of intentional meaning requires further explanation. That there are mental states with intentional attributes that mean (i) something cannot be an ultimate fact in ontology. And since the only plausible *explanans* is verbal behavior and linguistic meaning, then intentional meaning must, in some sense of analysis, be reducible to that. Such an argument must, of course, find a way of dealing with the undeniable fact that we do ascribe intentional meaning to nonhuman animals who lack the power of speech. It is not at all uncommon to ascribe thoughts, desires, and emotions to the brutes; surely a dog's belief that food is on its way cannot be rendered intelligible by reference to its speech dispositions. Here is the way Sellars tries to handle the problem:

> Not only do the subtle adjustments which animals make to their environment tempt us to say that they do what they do because they *believe* this, *desire* that, *expect* such and such, etc.; we are able to *explain* their behavior by ascribing to them these beliefs, desires, expectations, etc. But, and this is a key point, we invariably find ourselves *qualifying* these explanations in terms which would amount, in the case of a human subject, to the admission that he wasn't *really* thinking, believing, desiring, etc. For in the explanation of animal behavior the mentalistic framework is used as a *model* or *analogy* which is modified and restricted to fit the phenomena to be explained.[6]

6. Sellars, "Chisholm-Sellars Correspondence," p. 527.

Thus, Sellars argues, the fact that we do use mentalistic concepts for a reasonable purpose in describing and explaining animal behavior does not imply that intentional meaning really applies to the brutes; these concepts are applied analogically or metaphorically, and one of the things that is not carried over from their literal to their metaphorical use is intentional meaning.

In my view it is linguistic meaning that requires explanation, and intentional meaning is an indispensable component in an adequate explanation. Moreover, I suspect, although I cannot demonstrate, that intentional meaning is an ultimate fact in ontology. By this I do not mean that there can be no causal explanation for the emergence of mental states from material processes, for surely there can. What I do mean is that there cannot be a perspicuous and informative analysis of intentional meaning in other terms. Clearly this view cannot really be proved. The problem here is that the objector feels that intentional meaning is somehow unintelligible and that it needs to be explained. I agree. Ultimate facts in ontology are unintelligible in just the sense that, being ultimate, there is no further explanation of them; they cannot be accounted for. Moreover, intentional meaning needs to be explained in the sense that nothing but an explanation would render it intelligible. And, to this tautology I assent, merely adding that I do not think that any explanation will be forthcoming. So there really is no reply to this objection except to admit the premise and deny that it constitutes a real objection. There is, then, no need to refuse to ascribe intentional meaning to the brutes although ascribing it is not required by my view.

A second motive for adopting (2) and, perhaps (1), is the allegation that the view that I have espoused has a certain epistemological difficulty, namely, that one can never be sure what speech act, if any, a speaker is performing when he speaks a sentence. On the view that explains conventional meaning in terms of intentional meaning, in order to be able to identify a given linguistic action, one must be able to determine the G-S structure of the sentence spoken; but to be able to do this one must know the usual purposes for which the words and grammatical forms are employed; one must thus be able to determine the intentions of speakers independently of the words they use, and this, so the argument goes, is impossible. The only alternative is a nonpsychologistic view that explains conventional meaning without reference to mental states.

In order to rebut this objection, we must distinguish between the basis on which a person interprets another's linguistic actions and the method he would use to justify his system of interpretation. S says to L, "Le chat est sur le paillasson." L, who knows French well, interprets S as making the statement that the cat is on the mat. What does it mean for L, whose native language is English, to know French? This kind of knowledge is not theoretical; it is not necessary for L to be able to say what each word means and what the syntactic structures import. Sometime in his past L learned to associate certain French words and constructions with certain English ones. This past learning is a causal condition for his present ability to provide a correct interpretation of what S is saying. L's knowing French consists simply in his having this ability. Note that it is not an essential part of S's knowing French that he know the aims in the minds of Frenchmen, past and present, when they use words. What does it mean for L to know English? There is no difference between this case and the previous one. For him to know English is for him to be able to provide correct interpretations of the linguistic actions of native speakers. Of course, since English was his first language, the learning situation that created this ability was quite different; the specifics of his learning are not relevant now. The only point to mention is that his present ability does not depend upon any ability to recite how he learned English (something most of us do not remember) or to say what the standard aims of users of English are.

If L is a reflective person, then he might be interested in developing a theory of what is implied by the fact that he does know English. On the assumption that he really does know English, that is, that he usually gets his interpretations correct, he would, if he arrived at a theory like ours, find himself able to formulate statements about the standard aims and intentions of speakers of English when they use words. Statements about the mental states of English speakers are implied, on my view, by the fact that he knows English. But since a person does not and cannot know all the implications of what he does know, the fact that L knows that he knows English does not mean that he knows any of these facts about English speakers. Nor is there any necessity for him to know these things in order for him to provide correct interpretations.

My initial response to the argument is simply to deny that one must make difficult inferences about the aims of speakers as a condition for providing correct interpretations. At this point, however, the objector may undertake to defend himself by saying that it is, after all, logically possible for L to provide consistent interpretations of the speech of members of his linguistic community without his interpretations being correct. The evidence for this is a certain indeterminacy in translation.

7   Skepticism about Meaning

Indeterminacy of Translation

In his book *Word and Object* W. V. Quine has formulated
the skepticism implicit in the epistemological objection discussed in chapter 6 in terms of a view about the translation
of one language into another.[1] I shall call this view the *thesis
of indeterminacy*. The best way of approaching Quine's thesis
is to note that in Part I of this volume, I attempted to develop
a theory of analyzing and explaining our everyday imputations
of meanings to words and our everyday interpretations of
linguistic actions. In Quine's terms, I took for granted our
intuitive semantics. In explaining what he means by "intuitive" he says, "By an intuitive account I mean one in which
terms are used in habitual ways, without reflecting on how
they might be defined or what presuppositions they might
conceal."[2] In Part I, I tried to clarify the presuppositions of
intuitive semantics, and, in clarifying them, I endorsed them.
But when Quine denies that there is any "linguistically neutral
meaning" or that there is such a thing as an "intercultural
proposition or meaning," and when he asserts that "the
notion of there being a fixed, explicable, and as yet
unexplained meaning in the speaker's mind is gratuitous,"[3]
he can be interpreted as rejecting the presuppositions of intuitive semantics and hence intuitive semantics itself. In so

1. W. V. Quine, *Word and Object* (Cambridge, Mass.: MIT Press,
1964).
2. Ibid., p. 36n.
3. Ibid., pp. 76, 77, 160.

doing, he is rejecting a certain portion of common belief and usage.[4]

Very roughly, the thesis of indeterminacy says that on the basis of behavioral evidence, there is no way of uniquely specifying a translation for any given utterance. In order to formulate the thesis sharply, Quine envisages a case of radical translation in which a linguist is engaged in the "translation of a language of a hitherto untouched people."[5] The task of the linguist is to construct a manual or a dictionary of the new language that will enable him to translate any native sentence into a sentence or, in the case of ambiguity, sentences of English. The dictionary entries are called *analytical hypotheses*; translation is a matter of applying analytical hypotheses to the native sentences to form corresponding English ones. According to Quine, because the only relevant observations the linguist can make are of the behavior or actions of the natives and the context in which this behavior occurs, the only evidence he can ever have in favor of an analytical hypothesis is behavioral. What one learns when one observes the behavior of a speaker are his speech dispositions, that is, his "current dispositions to respond verbally to current stimulation," where stimulation is construed narrowly as the physical energies impinging upon the sense organs.[6] An important class of speech dis-

4. Thus he writes: "To accept intentional usage at face value is . . . to postulate translation relations as somehow objectively valid though indeterminate in principle relative to the totality of speech dispositions. Such postulation promises little gain in scientific insight if there is no better ground for it than that the supposed translation relations are presupposed by the vernacular of semantics and intention" (ibid., p. 221).

5. Ibid., p. 28.

6. Ibid., pp. 28, 31.

positions is represented by Quine in the notion of the *stimulus meaning* of a sentence for a speaker—this is the class of stimulations that would prompt his assent (*affirmative stimulus meaning*) or dissent (*negative stimulus meaning*) to the sentence.[7] Quine explicitly denies that stimulus meaning represents anything resembling meaning in intuitive semantics.[8] This latter notion of meaning, being mentalistic, cannot, Quine thinks, be reduced to behavioral terms.

With this notion of radical translation before us, let me cite two formulations of the thesis of indeterminacy:

> The thesis is then this: manuals for translating one language into another can be set up in divergent ways, all compatible with the totality of speech dispositions, yet incompatible with one another. In countless places they will diverge in giving, as their respective translations of a sentence of the one language, sentences of the other language which stand to each other in no plausible sort of equivalence however loose. The firmer the direct links of a sentence with nonverbal stimulations, of course, the less drastically its translations can diverge from one another from manual to manual.

> The indeterminacy that I mean . . . is that rival systems of analytical hypotheses can conform to all speech dispositions within each of the languages concerned yet dictate in countless cases, utterly disparate translations: not mere mutual paraphrases, but translations each of which would be excluded by the other system of translation. Two such translations might even be patently con-

7. Ibid., pp. 32-33.
8. Ibid., pp. 46, 66.

trary in truth value, provided there is no stimulation
that would encourage assent to either.[9]

Thus, according to Quine's thesis, it is possible for two linguists to end up with different manuals or dictionaries for
the same language such that the analytical hypotheses or
dictionary entries of each are consistent with all the behavioral evidence, and by using the dictionaries to translate a native sentence, one ends up with disparate translations. These translations would be disparate because, by
reference to the intuitive semantics of English, they say
different things. Therefore, "analytical hypotheses . . . are
not determinate functions of linguistic behavior," and they
"exceed anything implicit in any native's dispositions to
speech behavior."[10]

To illustrate the force of his thesis, Quine considers a
sentence that would be well-linked with nonverbal stimulation. The native sentence "Gavagai" is translated by the
linguist as "rabbit" because in every case in which he observed natives pointing at something and saying "Gavagai,"
it was a rabbit they were pointing at. But, says Quine,

> who knows but what the objects to which this term
> applies are not rabbits after all but mere stages, or
> brief temporal segments, of rabbits? In either event the
> stimulus situations that prompt assent to "Gavagai"
> would be the same as for "Rabbit."[11]

The same stimulus situation exists not only for translations
of "Gavagai" as "rabbit" or "rabbit-stage" but also for
"undetached rabbit part" and "rabbit fusion" and also
"rabbit-hood." The problem as Quine explains it is that

9. Ibid., pp. 27, 73-74.
10. Ibid., pp. 69, 70.
11. Ibid., pp. 51-52.

> "rabbit" is a term of divided reference. As such it can-
> not be mastered without mastering its principle of in-
> dividuation: where one rabbit leaves off and another
> begins. And this cannot be mastered by pure ostension,
> however persistent.[12]

Because principles of individuation are left undetermined
by stimulus meaning, the behavioral evidence does not itself differentiate between concrete and abstract and between singular and general terms. Of course, the linguist
will have to settle on one translation or another, but he
accomplishes this by settling, quite independently of the
behavioral evidence, on the meanings of those terms used
in individuating reference, such as identity and difference.

  If the thesis of indeterminacy is formulated in a hypothetical form—"If the evidence available to the linguist is restricted to what may be gained from the natives' behavior,
then there exists a translational indeterminacy"—it turns
out to be compatible both with behavioristic theories of
language and mind such as Quine's and also with various
mentalistic theories. The claim that behavioral propensities,
narrowly construed as dispositions to engage in observable
peripheral activity, cannot completely account for our intuitive semantic judgments has most often been made by
opponents of behaviorism.[13] The only important type of
theory in conflict with this hypothetical is a behaviorism
which claims that our everyday judgments about meaning
and mind can be logically analyzed without remainder

12. W. V. Quine, "Ontological Relativity," *Journal of Philosophy*
65 (April 4, 1968): 189.
13. See, for example, Brand Blanshard, *The Nature of Thought*
(London: Allen and Unwin, 1939), vol. 1, chap. 7, and Noam Chomsky's "Review of B. F. Skinner's *Verbal Behavior*," reprinted in Fodor
and Katz, *The Structure of Language*, pp. 547-78.

into statements about propensities to peripheral behavior.
But Quine is not putting forward a merely hypothetical
claim. His thesis of indeterminacy in the form he gives to
it involves two categorical assertions. The first is that (1)
there is no evidence available to the linguist other than behavioral. "All the objective data he has to go on are the
forces that he sees impinging on the native's surfaces and
the observable behavior, vocal and otherwise, of the native."[14]
The total evidence is observed peripheral behavior and stimulation. Assertion (1) implies that where rival translations
are put forward, all compatible with the behavioral evidence,
there is no scientific way of deciding which is the correct
one. Different sets of analytical hypotheses "could be tied
for first place on all theoretically accessible evidence."[15]
This does not imply, on Quine's view, that the rival hypotheses are differences that make no difference. That they are
different is revealed in distinctions in the resultant translations; rival hypotheses yield a "difference in net output,"
and, consequently, the claim that they are rivals makes
"clear empirical sense."[16] One might think, then, that
Quine is asserting a Kantian type of skepticism—that there
is a thing-in-itself (namely, the real meaning)—which happens
to be unknowable. But this is not his intent at all. As his
second categorical assertion Quine is saying that (2) for almost
all analytical hypotheses, with the exception, perhaps, of
those interpreting observation terms, there is no "objective matter to be right or wrong about."[17] His thesis asserts
not merely an epistemological but an ontological indeterminacy.

14. Quine, *Word and Object,* p. 28.
15. Ibid., p. 75.
16. Ibid., pp. 73, 79.
17. Ibid., p. 73.

What is the relation between translational indeterminacy conceived epistemologically, as in (1) and conceived ontologically, as in (2)? One might think that the former supports the assertion of the existence of the latter; it is characteristic of empiricists to claim that where evidence cannot resolve a disagreement, then there really is no disagreement, at least as to matters of fact; that is, there is no objective matter to be right or wrong about. But Quine's theory of science does not accord with traditional empiricism in this matter. Quine has often stated that theories in general are indeterminate with respect to experience,[18] but that the existence of epistemological indeterminacy is perfectly compatible with saying that to accept a theory is to accept it as being true or right or correct, even though that judgment may be revised in the light of future experience. In one place, after discussing the benefits that an acceptable theory brings with it, he says of these benefits that "we can hope for no surer touchstone of reality."[19] Moreover, he has explicitly noted that the case of radical translation partakes of this epistemological indeterminacy.

> To the same degree that radical translation of sentences is under-determined by the totality of dispositions to verbal behavior, our own theories and beliefs in general are under-determined by the totality of possible sensory evidence time without end.[20]

Therefore, we cannot say that in Quine's own terms (1) supports (2).

18. Ibid., p. 64; see also Part 6 of "Two Dogmas of Empiricism," in *From a Logical Point of View* (New York: Harper & Row, 1963), pp. 20-46.
19. W. V. Quine, *The Ways of Paradox and Other Essays* (New York: Random House, 1966), p. 241.
20. Quine, *Word and Object*, p. 78.

The real basis and import of (2) are to be gathered not
from Quine's epistemology but from his ontology. Assertion (2) is really an abbreviated form of certain ontological
claims. For one way in which (2) could be falsified is if
there were propositions that functioned as the meanings of
sentences. If different sentences could express the same propositions,

> we would then have to suppose that among all the al-
> ternative systems of analytical hypotheses of transla-
> tion which are compatible with the totality of disposi-
> tions to verbal behavior on the part of the speakers of
> two languages, some are "really" right and others wrong
> on behaviorally inscrutable grounds of propositional
> identity.[21]

Another way, Quine, thinks, in which (2) would be falsified
is if sentence-meanings could be interpreted as ideas in the
mind of the speaker.

> Uncritical semantics is the myth of a museum in which
> the exhibits are meanings and the words are labels. . . .
> When . . . we turn . . . toward a naturalistic view of lan-
> guage and a behavioral view of meaning, what we give
> up is not just the museum figure of speech. We give up an
> assurance of determinacy. Seen according to the museum
> myth, the words and sentences of a language have their
> determinate meanings. To discover the meanings of a
> native's words we may have to observe his behavior, but
> still the meanings of the words are supposed to be deter-
> minate in the native's *mind,* his mental museum, even in
> cases where behavioral criteria are powerless to discover
> them for us.[22]

21. Ibid., p. 206.
22. Quine, "Ontological Relativity," pp. 186-87.

The ontological indeterminacy asserted in (2) is equivalent to the denial of propositional and mentalistic theories of meaning. I agree with the rejection of the first theory but not with the second, so I cannot accept (2). As far as I can tell, the only support Quine provides for (2) is (1), and yet even within his own framework, he cannot, as we have seen, substantiate any such relation between them.

Even if we should cease to consider (2), nevertheless, thesis (1) is what really bears on our problem. The motive, if you remember, for raising the question of indeterminacy, is that translational indeterminacy appears to support the second, epistemological reason for rejecting the view that conventional meaning is due to intentional meaning. Here is how (1) is relevant. If, as I argued, an interpretation or a system of interpretations of a person's linguistic actions has implications about the mental states of the members of the speech community, then, if (1) is true, it becomes impossible to defend any such interpretation or system. In particular, one cannot know or have any good reason for believing that the set of analytical hypotheses that one has adopted is more correct than any of the other sets consistent with the behavioral evidence. One cannot know what anyone is saying. But this is absurd. Therefore, so the argument goes, one should give up psychologism. There would then be nothing inscrutable lying behind linguistic behavior and implicated in its interpretations; there would then be nothing that could not be known or at least believed with good reason. Psychologism can stand only if it does not yield any unknowables, any things-in-themselves. But (1) supports the argument that psychologism is guilty as suspected. Let us see, therefore, whether (1) can withstand a more searching scrutiny.

Epistemological Indeterminacy

The linguist will, sooner or later, settle upon one set of

analytical hypotheses as the manual he will use for interpreting the natives' speech. All of the others consistent
with the same evidence will be excluded. Therefore, the linguist must, if Quine's view is correct, employ certain nonevidential principles as the basis for his selection. One of them
is the principle of simplicity, which applies to all cases of
theory selection; various departures from behavioral cor-
respondences are licensed on the grounds of avoiding com-
plicated analytical hypotheses.[23] But it is the principles
specific to the problem of translation that I shall focus upon.
First, note that if a principle or a fact is employed as evidence
in favor of some hypothesis, then it constitutes a reason or a
part of a reason for accepting that hypothesis as true. But if
a principle is nonevidential, then even if it is used to choose
among rival theories, it provides no reason or part of a reason
for thinking that the hypothesis selected is true. Thus a choice
made by the use of nonevidential principles is, in a sense, arbitrary, even though, to the one who makes it, it may appear
natural and even necessitated.

Quine does tell us how he thinks the linguist would make
his selection among competing hypotheses. In one place he
remarks that the linguist might yet translate "Gavagai" as
"rabbit" even if there were some differences in their stimulus meanings because "he translates not by identity of stimulus meanings, but by significant approximation of stimulus
meanings." In ignoring minor differences, the linguist, says
Quine, "is influenced by his natural expectation that any
people in rabbit country would have *some* brief expression
that could in the long run be best translated simply as 'Rabbit.' "[24] A natural principle for this case could be formulated
roughly as: (a) If a discriminable physical object occurs often

23. Quine, *Word and Object*, p. 67.
24. Ibid., p. 40.

in the environment of a group of people, and if the object is of interest to them (for example, they use it or eat it or worship it), then very probably their language will contain a word or brief expression for that object. Quine formulates a principle very much like (a) but using the language of gestalt psychology: (b) "the more conspicuously segregated wholes are likelier to bear the simpler terms."[25] In another place he reformulates (b) as "an enduring and relatively homogenous object, moving as a whole against a contrasting background, is a likely reference for a short expression."[26]

In still another place, the linguist is said to project his own linguistic habits in formulating hypotheses about the syntactic structure of native sentences.[27] The principle here could be formulated as: (c) languages spoken by human beings and readily learned by them will have many similar syntactical devices. Finally, the linguist is said to impose his own logic— "fair translation preserves logical laws"[28]—in order to avoid translating a seriously meant native sentence as an obvious contradiction or logical error. The principle here is: (d) people do not usually believe explicit contradictions.

According to (1), principles (a), (b), (c), and (d) are nonevidential because (1) asserts that the only evidence available consists in knowledge of the impinging stimuli and the natives' reaction, that is, stimulus meaning. Quine says little to justify their exclusion from the evidential base. He denies, without any accompanying argument, that (b) is "a substantive law of speech behavior."[29] Of the linguist's use of (b) Quine remarks:

25. Ibid., p. 74.
26. Quine, "Ontological Relativity," p. 191.
27. Quine, *Word and Object,* p. 70.
28. Ibid., p. 59.
29. Ibid., p. 74.

> If he were to become conscious of this maxim, he might
> well celebrate it as one of the linguistic universals, or traits
> of all languages, and he would have no trouble pointing
> out its psychological plausibility. But he would be wrong,
> the maxim is his own imposition, toward the settling
> what is objectively indeterminate."[30]

This comment does follow from (2), but we have seen no
reason to accept it.

It is odd to think of (a)-(d) as being nonevidential, as if
there were no evidence to support their use. If there were
or could be evidence in their favor, then they would constitute
reasons for thinking that one set of analytical hypotheses
was more correct than its rivals. The queston is not whether
(a)-(d) are true or whether there actually is any evidence in
their favor, but whether they are specimens of a type of
principle that could be evidential and that could reduce the
indeterminacy. For if they are, then (1) would turn out to
be false, and the linguist would not be restricted to stimulus
meaning. Though these principles are rough generalizations,
lacking the precision of many scientific laws, they are no
worse than many other generalizations that we rely on and
for which we have strong evidence such as: "Things usually
fall when dropped"; "Iron bars are hard to bend with bare
hands"; "Wooden objects float." Such "laws" are liable to
exceptions; they hold "for the most part" and are useful
and well substantiated. For the purpose of precise investigation or for actions requiring precise knowledge, they are
capable of refinement, qualification, and restriction in scope.

Principles like (a) and (b) have been put forward in the
literature of psychology as hypotheses confirmable by scientific techniques.[31] Gestalt psychologists have argued that

---

30. Quine, "Ontological Relativity," p. 191.

prior to the acquisition of language, perceptual experience exemplifies to some extent the objectlike structure it has for adults,[32] thus making it plausible that numerous items in the vocabulary of any natural language will represent physical things, their properties, and relations. Since these principles are specimens of a type that are of great interest in psychological investigation, it is strange that Quine describes their employment by the linguist engaged in radical translation as his "own imposition" in contrast to generalizations having evidential support. Perhaps Quine has the following argument in mind. These principles and others like them can be confirmed by experiments and surveys in which the experimenter uses subjects who speak his language. Because he belongs to their linguistic community, he can understand and consequently rely upon their reports about what they perceive, or mean, or believe on various occasions. Take (d) as an example. If a person utters a sentence having the grammatical form "p and not p," such as "It is raining and it is not raining," we can request him to paraphrase his utterance by using another sentence. If, in such cases, the paraphrases turn out to be logically consistent, then we can justifiably infer that the originals were merely *façons de parler* and not really contradictions. In this way, (d) is initially confirmed with its scope limited to persons of the same language community as the experimenter. If he were to try to extend its scope to persons speaking a different langauge, he would first have to learn that language in order to elicit and interpret the experimental data. It follows that in order to justify extending (d), he must settle upon some system of analytical hypoth-

31. See, for example, Jerome Bruner, "On Perceptual Readiness," *Readings in Perception,* ed. David C. Beardslee and Michael Wertheimer (New York: Van Nostrand, 1958), esp. p. 699.

32. Kurt Koffka, *The Growth of the Mind* (Totowa, N.J.: Littlefield, 1959), p. 342.

eses as the very condition of testing it in the new circumstances. He would have no right, therefore, to claim that his use of (d) to select analytical hypotheses is based upon evidence because the evidence does not come until later. According to this argument, it is not that (a)-(d) are inherently nonevidential principles; it is rather that in the particular circumstances in which they are used in radical translation, their employment is not susceptible of justification by evidence.

The question is, then, whether (a)-(d) can be justifiably extrapolated from one's own language community to another in radical translation—whether there is evidence to justify the extrapolation that can be gathered independently of the choice of a set of analytical hypotheses used to interpret the new language. Let us restrict our attention to (b) in taking up this question. We shall suppose that we can, in a rough way, compare objects frequently occurring in the environment of a people who speak our language with respect to their degree of perceptual distinguishability and segregation. We shall also suppose that we discover that objects possessed of a high degree of distinguishability are more likely to be named by a short word or brief expression than objects with a low degree of distinguishability. In these circumstances (b) would be confirmed for our language community at least. Let us further suppose that (b) can be explained by reference to some underlying physiological mechanism, perhaps a mechanism exemplifying a law of "least action" in the nervous system. And finally we suppose that the mechanism is found to be species invariant—it is discovered to be present in all normal human beings by means of physiological research conducted independently of introspective reports. What has been supposed is that a familiar type of psychological program is realized, namely, that an underlying physiological mechanism is found to explain inductively established psychological and psycholinguistic correlations. The existence of such circumstances is surely an abstract possibility. But if they should turn out to be real, we would then have evidence, obtained without begging the question, which would justify using (b), in addition to the behavioral evidence, to reduce the indeterminacy. It seems, then, that there are arguments against (1), the assertion that there is no evidence available to the linguist other than behavioral.

A reason that Quine gives in favor of (1) suggests the kind of response he might be inclined to give to this sort or criticism.

> Language is a social art. In acquiring it we have to depend entirely on intersubjectively available cues as to what to say and when. Hence there is no justification for collating linguistic meanings, unless in terms of men's dispositions to respond overtly to socially observable stimulations. An effect of recognizing this limitation is that the enterprise of translation is found to be involved in a certain systematic indeterminacy.[33]

This argument assumes that when a child is learning a language in the usual way, he must depend solely on the behavioral evidence for collating linguistic meanings. Since the restriction to behavioral evidence represents the natural condition under which languages are learned, then the linguist, engaged in radical translation, must accept this restriction as well because it is his task to reproduce what the child learns. This assumption, however, begs the question at issue. The child may very well be using (a)-(d) or similar principles in the form of innate mechanisms of interpretation; later investigation into species invariant psychological

33. Quine, *Word and Object,* p. ix.

and physiological traits may establish that their use can be justified by evidence.

There is, therefore, no reason to think that the epistemological indeterminacy implied by (1) really exists. It is likely that the inference from behavioral evidence to the analytical hypotheses is mediated by hypotheses referring to underlying physiological and/or psychological mechanisms. In those cases in which one's interpretations of another's linguistic actions seem so natural as not to require inference or thought, as when one understands the speech of another who is talking in one's own language, one's use of principles (a)-(d) is habitual and may perhaps be explained as being caused by innate mechanisms of interpretation. Therefore, the second argument supporting Sellars's denial that conventional meaning is due to intentional meaning fails.[34]

34. My discussion and critique of the thesis of indeterminacy has assumed the validity of processes of theoretical inference from observable phenomena to unobservable entities postulated to explain them. I have merely suggested how theoretical inference might be employed in avoiding the restriction to stimulus meaning. One might, perhaps, wish to defend the thesis by invoking a general form of skepticism concerning our knowledge of other minds. There is evidence that Quine resorts to this occasionally (see *Word and Object*, p. 71). Because a general skepticism throws doubt upon so much of our common belief, it is not specific to the case of radical translation and may be put aside in this context.

8 Universals

Predication

In chapter 5 there was a brief discussion of the subordinate
linguistic action of qualification in which a person uses a
sentence to ascribe a quality to some object. The simplest
type of sentence used in qualification is of the subject-
predicate form such as "O is green" where the subject-term
"O" singles out a certain object, and the predicate-term
"green" is used to ascribe a quality to it. Because the function of qualification is so often performed by the predicate-
term, it has often been called *predication*. I shall use both
these labels interchangeably. Predication has excited more
discussion in the history of logic than any other linguistic
function because it is one of the simplest ways in which
general terms are used, and it is reflection upon the use of
general terms that has generated the problem of *universals*.
This problem has often been formulated as the attempt to
find an explanation of the fact that the same word can be
used to apply to many things.

The first question to consider is how, in the light of the
approach developed in Part I, the word "green" in its adjectival uses stands in relation to the color green. The answer
is quite simple. In delineating the various uses of "green,"
the color green was mentioned in all of them: thus "green"
is used to ascribe the color green to an object or to deny
the color green to an object or to describe an object as having
the color green, and so on. This complex fact about how
"green" stands with respect to the color green can be abbreviated by the formula " 'Green' means green." Let us say,
as a way of stating this fact, that the word "green" signifies
the color green. More generally, any general term that has to

a quality of or relation among objects the connection that "green" has to green will be said to *signify* that quality or relation. And the quality or relation will be said to be the *signification* of the term.

To understand this notion of signification, let us start by considering the view that signifying is identical with what some philosophies have called naming or referring. In the sentence

(1) This leaf is green.

the subject-term "this leaf" is used to identify or pick out that object to which the predicate "green" is applied. When a singular term such as "this leaf" is used in this way, let us say that it refers to or names that object, and let us stipulate that the object must exist in order for the term to be a name. If the object fails to exist, as in "Pegasus is a winged horse," then we shall say, not that the word "Pegasus" is a name, but that it is a pseudo-name. Pseudo-names are just like names except that there exists no object which they name. Is the word "green" in (1) a name? It is not a noun or a noun phrase, but I have not stipulated in advance that names must belong to any special grammatical category. There is, however, an argument that justifies a negative answer to the question. For the sake of the argument let us suppose that (1) is used to make a true statement. Let us also suppose that in (1)

(2) "Green" is a name of the quality green.

Note that the phrase "the quality green" is also a name of green. Thus,

(3) "Green" and "the quality green" are names of the same thing.

There is a rule of inference—the *law of substitutivity*—according to which words that name the same thing can be substituted for one another in sentences in which they occur without changing the truth-value of the statements that these sentences are used to make.[1] Consequently, according to (3) we can substitute in (1) the phrase "the quality green" for "green," and we come up with

(4) This leaf is the quality green.

But (4) is either absurd or false. It is false if the copula "is" functions to signify the relation of identity, for this leaf is certainly not identical with the color green. And it is absurd or without plausible interpretation if the copula functions to introduce predication. What went wrong? Neither the truth of (1) nor the validity of the law of substitutivity is in question here. And (3) is derivative from (2). So the crucial error is in accepting (2). But since the same argument could apply to any adjectival expression occurring in the predicate, that (2) is erroneous establishes that signifying is not the same function as naming.

To this argument Gustav Bergmann has replied that in replacing "green" by "the quality green" in (1), it is also necessary to replace the copula by "exemplifies."[2] This gives us

(5) This leaf exemplifies the quality green,

which is true, provided (1) is. In effect Bergmann is saying that the error in the original substitution, which yielded (4), was due to the law of substitutivity. This law should be amended to require the replacement of the copula by "exemplifies" to accompany substitutions for the predicate.

1. There have been doubts raised as to whether the law of substitutivity holds unreservedly. I think these doubts are unjustified. But the context in which the law is used in this discussion is not among those for which doubts have arisen.

2. Gustav Bergmann, *Meaning and Existence* (Madison, Wis.: University of Wisconsin Press, 1960), p. 220.

Bergmann's argument sounds like an ad hoc intervention to save a theory—and the theory that he is trying to save by this gambit is realism.

> In the strict sense an ontologist is a realist if he counts characters, or at least some characters (for example, simple ones), as a kind of existent. A nominalist in the strict sense holds, conversely, that no characters are existents.[3]

He offers an account of predication that he thinks is required by realism. Of the sentence "Peter is blond" he says:

> "Peter" and "blond" both stand for existents. . . . Many realists, including myself, also hold that every existent is either an individual or a character. . . . What "Peter is blond" stands for comes about if two existents, one of each kind, enter into a certain "relation," or, as I would rather say, nexus. This nexus the realist calls *exemplification.* . . . The copula or, as I prefer to say, the predicative "is" stands for exemplification.[4]

However, it is not sufficient, in order to defend realism, to insist that "blond" functions as a name of a character just as "Peter" functions as a name of a person. For since pseudo-names are just like names except that in the case of the latter there exists an entity that is named, a consideration of linguistic functions as such would not be sufficient to establish that "blond" is a name rather than a pseudo-name and thus would not be sufficient to establish realism. Moreover, such a defense is not even necessary, for any consideration that would establish that there must exist an entity named by "blond" would also establish that there must be one signified

3. Ibid., p. 206.
4. Ibid., p. 208.

by that word. So there is no reason in defending realism to try to reduce signifying to naming.

Is signifying a relation between a word on the one hand and a quality or relation on the other? If it is, then whatever a word signifies must exist. And since talk about signifying is merely abbreviated discourse about the various uses of a word, and since these uses constitute the word's meaning, then, if signifying were a relation, merely knowing the meaning of a word would be sufficient to establish the existence of certain entities. It is for this reason that philosophers have claimed to be able to generate an ontology from a semantical theory.[5]

I want to deny that signifying is a relation. In formulating the reason, instead of taking an example like (1) in which the predicate is adjectival, I shall use a sentence in which the predicate is a substantive, such as

(6) That animal is a horse.

For the same reason that I said that "green" signifies the color green, I want to claim that "horse" as used predicatively signifies the species horse and that other substantives used predicatively signify species or kinds. We often have occasion to speak of the existence of a species. Of a species whose members are dying faster than they are being replaced, we say that it is in danger of going out of existence. We also allow that the evolutionary process may bring new species into existence. It is clear that in this mode of discourse a necessary and sufficient condition for the existence of a species is that there exists at least one member of it. The species horse exists because there is at least one horse, and if all

5. See Rudolf Carnap, "Empiricism, Semantics, and Ontology," in *Meaning and Necessity*, 2d ed. (Chicago: University of Chicago Press, 1956), pp. 205-21.

horses suddenly died out, the species would cease to exist. The species centaur does not exist because there are no centaurs. Certainly one could understand what type of statement could be made by (6) given its G-S structure without knowing whether there actually exist any horses, just as one could understand

(7) That animal is a centaur

or

(8) That animal is a dragon,

without having firm opinions about the existence of centaurs or dragons. In fact one could understand (7) and (8) knowing that there are no centaurs and dragons. It follows, since "centaur" signifies the species centaur and "dragon" the species dragon, that signifying does not establish the existence of the signification. Thus in the case of species or kinds, signifying is not a relation. Now I submit that quality and relation words can be treated like species words. In order for the color blue to exist, there must be at least one blue thing. In order for the relation of fatherhood to exist, there must be at least two persons such that one is the father of the other. Thus the fact that "green" signifies the color green in (1) does not establish the existence of the color green. In general, then, one cannot establish points in ontology from linguistic facts about words, such as their functioning as names or as signifiers.[6]

6. There are alternative definitions of the existence of qualities, relations and species; for example—a character exists if there is no inconsistency in the supposition that it has instances. In this case consistent signifying would establish existence. But since "existence" means something different in this definition and mine, there is no conflict between the two views about signifying. Nor do I think my definition to be the only correct one, since I doubt that there is any reason for competition here.

According to what I have just said, if (1) is true, that would establish the existence of the color green because it would verify the existence of one thing having that color. And if (6) is true, that would establish the existence of the species horse. Does this mean that certain evident truths of these types are sufficient to demonstrate the truth of realism and the falsehood of nominalism? Does the fact that I can now make a true statement using (1) prove that Bergmann's ontology is correct and Hobbes's incorrect? Of course not. That would be too facile a way of doing ontology and would fail to explain the nature, the length, and the intensity of the dispute.

Ontology and the Problem of Universals

The traditional problem of universals begins with reflection upon the fact that there is recurrence or repetition in nature. The same colors, shapes, and sounds occur over and over again. We are continuously presented not only with novel things but with qualities and features of things that we have observed innumerable times before. And even the novel things very often belong to types—that is, to species and genera—that are quite familiar. As an example of natural recurrence, consider two leaves that are exactly alike in all their qualities: they have the same green color, the exact same shape, size, and feel. There is no difficulty in distinguishing among their qualities; a color, after all, is not a shape, a shape not a size; in other objects the same color coexists with different shapes, the same shapes with different sizes. In addition, there is an evident distinction between any one of the qualities and the thing itself—the leaf—which possesses it; we can distinguish between the leaf and its shape and color by imagining changes in quality—the color turning from green to brown in autumn or the shape being modified by a storm—though the object remains the same. The distinction between a particular thing and its qualities is well entrenched in our everyday thinking and speaking about the world. Things persist through space and time; qualities repeat themselves in different things at various times and places.

The phenomenon of natural recurrence seems easily explained; it consists in the fact that different objects have qualities in common; our two leaves, for example, have their color, shape, and size in common. It is the existence of common qualities that allows us to say that recurrence is literally repetition; the same quality literally appears over and over again. Common qualities have been given the technical name "universals" because of the fact that they are repeatable and can be possessed by diverse things. The spatiotemporal things that have the qualities are often called *particulars* or *individuals* or *concrete entities*; these are not repeatable in exactly the same way that universals are; no particular can be in totally different places at the same time, whereas a universal such as a shade of color is subject to no such restrictions. The explanation of natural recurrence in terms of common qualities or universals I shall call the theory of universals; it is also often called *realism* because it asserts that universals are real. The opposed type of view, which tries to get by without universals, I shall call *particularism*.[7]

It may be thought that the explanation of natural recurrence in terms of common qualities consists of a series of truisms that no reasonable man would want to deny. Never-

7. The terminology of metaphysics is not standardized; different philosophers have given different titles to the views they espouse or oppose. Other terms for realism are "Platonism" and "the identity theory." The term "nominalism" is often used instead of "particularism," but I shall use it later to designate one form that particularism can assume.

theless, at the very beginning of the Western philosophical tradition, Plato found that these truisms led to certain puzzles. In his dialogue *Parmenides,* Parmenides receives an affirmative answer from Socrates to this question:

> But I should like to know whether you mean that there are certain ideas of which all other things partake, and from which they derive their names; that similars, for example, become similar, because they partake of similarity; and great things become great, because they partake of greatness; and that just and beautiful things become just and beautiful, because they partake of justice and beauty?

In this and other passages the Platonic ideas can be interpreted as common qualities; a thing that has a certain quality is said to partake of or participate in the corresponding idea. Parmenides then proceeds to find difficulties in Socrates' theory. One difficulty is especially relevant to the notion of a common quality.

> Then each individual partakes either of the whole of the idea or else of a part of the idea? Can there be any other mode of participation?
>
> There cannot be, Socrates said.
>
> Then do you think that the whole idea is one, and yet, being one, is in each one of the many?
>
> Why not, Parmenides? said Socrates.
>
> Because one and the same thing will exist as a whole at the same time in many separate individuals, and will therefore be in a state of separation from itself.
>
> Nay, but the idea may be like the day which is one and the same in many places at once, and yet continuous with

itself; in this way each idea may be one and the same in all at the same time.

I like your way, Socrates, of making one in many places at once. You mean to say, that if I were to spread out a sail and cover a number of men, there would be one whole including many—is not that your meaning?

I think so.

And would you say that the whole sail includes each man, or a part of it only, and different parts different men?

The latter.

Then, Socrates, the ideas themselves will be divisible, and things which participate in them will have a part of them only and not the whole idea existing in each of them?

That seems to follow.

Then would you like to say, Socrates, that the one idea is really divisible and yet remains one?

Certainly not, he said.

Suppose you divide absolute greatness, and that of the many great things, each one is great in virtue of a portion of greatness less than absolute greatness—is that conceivable?

No. . . .

Then in what way, Socrates, will all things participate in the ideas, if they are unable to participate in them either as parts or wholes?[8]

---

8. Plato, *Parmenides* (tr. Jowett), 131.

Parmenides' argument takes the form of a dilemma. In the example, the two leaves are both green. There are two alternatives for understanding this fact in terms of common qualities. Either the color green is possessed by each leaf as a whole, or each possesses only a part of the color. But each alternative is absurd. The first is absurd because it implies that the same entity, the color green, can be in different and separated places at the same time, that it will be "in a state of separation from itself." The second is absurd because it is unintelligible how something can be green by possessing not the quality green but only a part of the quality: it is not even clear what a part of a simple quality like green can be.

The fact that realism is still a living option proves that philosophers have not taken Parmenides' argument to be conclusive. Realists almost invariably accept the first alternative, that the color is possessed by each leaf as a whole. There are, however, at least two distinct strategies for rebutting the claim that this leads to an absurdity. According to the first, the realist denies that the statement that the same color can be in two or more places at once follows from the fact that the color is possessed by each leaf as a whole; he insists that universals do not have spatiotemporal location at all except indirectly, via the particulars that participate in them. It does not make sense, he says, to raise such questions as: Where is the color green now? Where was it yesterday?

The second strategy is to accept the implication that colors can be in two or more places at once and to deny that this is absurd or false. The supposition that this is absurd comes from confusing qualities with particulars. If a particular A and a particular B occupy distinct and separate places at the same time, this proves that A and

B are different. There is no reason, however, to apply this criterion of difference to qualities.

With this strategy we have invoked a kind of argument that appears over and over in ontology—a *category explanation*. The question was raised: How can the color green be in two different places at the same time? The answer given by realism is that green, being a quality, is not subject to the criterion of spatial separation as a basis of difference. This answer first specifies the category or ontological type to which green belongs and then points out that certain things are or fail to be true of it because it belongs to this type. In general, a category explanation of the question: How can some entity A have the feature F? has the form: A belongs to category C, and its belonging to C implies that it has F.

Someone might argue that a category explanation is not a final answer to the question, since one can always ask how it is that something has F just because it belongs to C. The response to this is that to raise this further question is like asking: How is it that something is colored just because it is green? or How is it that something is rectangular just because it is square? There are no answers to these questions other than pointing out that given what these things are, these relationships hold. Of course one is always free to deny that something presented as a category explanation really is such and to present metaphysical arguments to support his denial.

Realism, then, can defend itself against certain fundamental objections. The problem of universals, or at least one form of it, can be described as the question whether realism provides an adequate account of natural recurrence. As it stands, however, the theory of universals hardly seems worthy of being classified as a theory. Despite the apparent difficulties that Parmenides found in it, it seems to consist of obvious truisms expressed in a somewhat technical vocabulary. Who can deny that things can possess qualities in common, that many things can be red or green or square at the same time? The claim that this truism is a metaphysical theory strikes one as a bit pretentious. And to say that it is an answer to a problem seems at variance with our usual conception of a problem, namely, a question difficult to answer. Nevertheless, I do not think that realism is an uninteresting truism, and I do think that there really is a problem of universals. It is therefore necessary to consider further what is involved in the claim of realism.

The Problem of Universals Vindicated

The problem of universals, as I originally formulated it, arose as an attempt to explain natural recurrence. It is, of course, important to distinguish our description of the phenomenon to be explained—natural recurrence—from an explanation of it—say, the theory of universals. It is not easy to keep these things separate, since almost any set of terms we use to point out the phenomenon of natural recurrence suggests one of the explanatory theories; the description and explanation may be formulated in the same vocabulary. For example, in indicating what I meant by natural recurrence in the first place, I used the vocabulary of common qualities, and thus my description was linguistically indistinguishable from the theory of universals. But there are other terms I could have used to identify natural recurrence; I could have said, not that things have qualities in common, but that they resemble one another to a great degree; or instead of speaking of qualities or resemblances, I could have mentioned the fact of *linguistic recurrence*, namely, that we often apply the same word to different things.

Natural recurrence is something presented to us in our

sense experience. That there is such a thing is a truism; it is that which various ontologies try to explain. Realism or the theory of universals is not itself to be identified with the assertion of the existence of natural recurrence but is rather one account of it. The situation resembles that in the sciences when the very phenomenon to be explained tends to be identified in terms of a current explanatory theory. To take an example from psychology, there are several theories attempting to explain mental illness. But the very term "mental illness" already implies a certain theoretical and practical point of view. A psychologist who rejects the point of view would naturally refuse to use the term "mental illness" to identify what he wants to explain; he will have to use another term such as "behavior problem" to indicate what he is after. If he should say that there is no such thing as mental illness, it sounds as if he is speaking a paradox although, in fact, he is rejecting the theory, not the phenomenon. Similarly a philosopher who refuses to accept the theory of universals is not necessarily denying that there is such a thing as natural recurrence although he may wish to describe it in terms that suggest a different theory.

This account will not yet satisfy the skeptic who insists that the theory of universals is an uninteresting truism. He will respond that, even considered as an explanation of natural recurrence, one cannot sensibly deny that different things are square because each possesses the shape square. That there is such a thing as the color red in virtue of which all red things are red can be ascertained just by opening one's eyes and looking. This is hardly a contentious point but is rather a straightforward empirical fact.

In order to reply to this argument of the skeptic, it is necessary to introduce another distinction, namely, one between commonsensical and philosophical claims of existence. In everyday discourse such sentences as "The red color of

that book is darker than the red color of this table" and
"Both these leaves possess the same shape" may be used to
make true statements that imply or presuppose the existence
of colors and shapes. But these commonsense existence
claims do not yet constitute a philosophical theory, nor are
they of any value to metaphysics except as data for reflection. A philosopher may claim that statements which mention certain types of entity, such as qualities, and ostensibly
presuppose their existence may, for all rational purposes,
be replaced by statements that do not mention them but
that mention, say, only resemblances among particulars.
If he can make such a claim, then he is entitled to assert
that, in a sense, there are no such things as qualities, only
particulars and resemblances among them. In general, if a
philosopher can show that things of type A are reducible
to or replaceable by things of type B, that A's are nothing
but B's, or that statements which mention things of type A
are translatable into statements which mention only things
of type B, he is then entitled to say that, in a sense, things
of type A do not exist, but things of type B do.

In a philosophical system the types of entities out of
which all other types are "composed" are the system's *ultimate categories*. A philosophical existence statement asserts
the existence of members of the ultimate categories. The
statement that qualities (for example, colors and shapes)
exist, if it is intended as a commonsense existence statement, does not contradict the statement that qualities do
not exist if that is intended as the claim that qualities are
not an ultimate category. From the point of view of this
philosophical claim, our commonsense reference to qualities
is a mere manner of speaking, which can be dispensed with
for philosophical purposes. The statements that the skeptic
finds to be uninteresting truisms are not the ones that the
philosopher asserts; those that the philosopher does assert,

though very often compatible with commonsense existence claims, are not identical with them.

At various points in this discussion I have made use of the notion of *metaphysical explanation,* and this may now become the target of the skeptic's doubts. There are various sorts of explanation employed in everyday life and in the sciences. We often explain how a phenomenon came about by mentioning one of its causes, or we may explain why a person did something by citing his motives or reasons. That there is something more we can do with a phenomenon, such as providing a metaphysical account of it, is problematic. Once we have stated something's causes or its reasons, what else, asks the skeptic, is there to know about it that a further explanation would accomplish?

One source of resistance to the notion of a metaphysical explanation is that such explanations are often couched in terms that make them appear as if they were rivals to the causal explanations encountered in everyday life and science. In the passage of Plato quoted earlier, there occurs the sentence "Just and beautiful things become just and beautiful, because they partake of justice and beauty." This sounds as if Plato were offering a causal explanation of how things become just or beautiful. Yet if we really wanted instructions as to how to make a person just or to make a painting beautiful, what Plato wrote would be useless. The metaphysical explanation sounds like a form of primitive science, which could now be replaced by the sophisticated methods of modern science. Thus David Pears has written:

> "Because universals exist" is the answer to at least two general questions: "Why are things what they are?" and "Why are we able to name things as we do?" Though Plato and Aristotle sometimes distinguished these two questions, it was characteristic of Greek thought to con-

fuse them. Yet they can be clearly distinguished, the
first requiring a dynamic answer from scientists, and
the second a static answer from logicians. Now philosophy has often staked premature claims in the terri-
tory of science by giving quick comprehensive answers
to questions which really required laborious detailed
answers. And clearly this is what happened to the first
of the two questions. When detailed causal answers
were provided to it, the comprehensive answer "Because universals exist" was no longer acceptable or
necessary.[9]

In the opinion of skeptics like Pears, science has replaced
metaphysics and has shown it to be superfluous. This skepticism would be correct if its understanding of the function
of metaphysics is correct; only if metaphysics has the
same explanatory function as science, could one claim that
science has replaced metaphysics. But if metaphysics can
be shown to be doing something different from science, if
its explanations can be shown not to be rivals of those provided by science, then this criticism misses the target.

What then is a metaphysical explanation? The theory of
universals illustrates one way of answering this question. It
attempts to account for a general feature of our experience—
natural recurrence—by stating the entities which that feature
consists of—universals occurring in diverse particulars—where
the entities are classified in terms of ultimate categories. In
general, a metaphysical account is a redescription of some
general and pervasive features of our experience and of the
world in terms of ultimate categories. These redescriptions
are not rival causal explanations; they are not alternative to

9. David F. Pears, "Universals," reprinted in *Logic and Language*,
ed. A. G. N. Flew, Second Series (Oxford: Blackwell, 1955), p. 52.

the accounts provided by science; they give not antecedent causes, but the ultimate categories from which the world is constituted. It is in this way that metaphysics tells us about the nature of reality.

If realism is to be a theory worth asserting, it must also be worth denying, and this means that there must be rival accounts of natural recurrence. There is a form of skepticism about metaphysics according to which different theories are not really rivals at all; they are merely distinct though compatible redescriptions of the world. The choice among them is not to be based on evidence showing one to be true and the others false, because they are all equally true. It is to be based rather upon such things as aesthetic preference or verbal utility. This skepticism is often engendered by noticing the length of time various metaphysical theories have endured in the history of philosophy and the apparent difficulty of proving one and refuting others. This difficulty is explained by supposing that the need to prove and refute is a mere illusion.

In order to rebut this form of skepticism it is sufficient to provide formulations of various metaphysical explanations of natural recurrence that are logically incompatible with one another. Since natural recurrence consists in the recurrence of qualities, each explanation will be a theory about the nature of qualities. We can identify the sort of thing the various theories are about by pointing—either verbally or by gesture—to examples of them. For instance, take any physical object and point to its color or its shape; these are the sorts of thing meant by "quality."[10] Realism asserts that qualities are universals; this can be interpreted

10. Even nominalism, which, as will be explained below, denies the existence of qualities, can concede the truth of these everyday existence claims.

as an identity criterion for qualities, namely, as the assertion that there are cases of A being identical with B or of A being numerically the same as B when A and B are qualities of different objects at the same time.

This formulation of the theory of universals suggests a way of specifying an alternative account, which I shall call the *theory of abstract particulars*.[11] It says that when A and B are qualities of different objects, it follows that A is not identical with B. In the words of G. F. Stout, qualities are abstract particulars; they are as particular as the things they qualify. The theory of universals and the theory of abstract particulars are rivals in this precise sense: although both accept quality as an ultimate category, the former asserts and the latter denies a certain identity criterion for qualities. These theories are saying different and logically incompatible things about the same thing. But how can we be sure they are both about the same thing? Our assurance is based upon the fact that what they are about has been identified in a neutral way. Through an everyday type of existence claim we were able to point out and call attention to examples of what these theories are about—colors and shapes— in a manner that does not commit the person who does the pointing or the one who interprets it either to the view that quality is an ultimate category or to any specific identity criterion for qualities.

This analysis yields another way in which metaphysical theories can be rivals. Instead of merely disagreeing about the identity conditions of some ultimate category, a philosopher may deny that this is an ultimate category in the first place; he may assert that there are no such things as

11. This theory is identified especially with G. F. Stout. See his article "The Nature of Universals and Propositions," in *Studies in Philosophy and Psychology* (London: Macmillan, 1930), chap. 17.

qualities. And this is what several other forms of particularism do.[12]

According to nominalism, natural recurrence consists simply of linguistic recurrence—the fact that the same word can be applied to diverse particulars. Nominalism reduces qualities to general words in the sense that the fact that two different things have the same quality consists of the fact that the same word applies to both of them. For the nominalist, general words are not construed as names of qualities; they are not names at all. Rather they are applied to or predicated of the particulars that are commonsensically said to have the quality signified by the general word. Consequently, for nominalism, the use of a general word does not presuppose the existence of qualities.

Another version of particularism that rejects the category of quality is the resemblance theory. On this view there exists an objective basis for applying general words to diverse particulars, namely, the resemblances among them. We apply "green" to various things because they resemble one another in being green; we apply "square" to those things that resemble one another in being square. The resemblance theory could be looked upon as a mere corollary to nominalism. But it could also be formulated as a rival in this way: Suppose a philosopher thinks that the use of a general term in a sentence such as "This leaf is green" commits the user to the existence of qualities, but being a particularist he wants to avoid a metaphysical commitment to qualities. He might then claim that this sentence can be translated into another that does not presuppose qualities. For example, select some green object as an exemplar of green; call the exemplar "A"; then "This leaf is green" be-

12. The theory of abstract particulars is a form of particularism.

comes something like "This leaf resembles A." Qualities then are reduced to resembling particulars. The nominalist, having a different view of the use of general terms, finds no need for such a reduction. In any case we now have four theories—realism and three forms of particularism that can be formulated so as to imply or presuppose logically incompatible theses.

9   In Defense of Realism

Realism versus Nominalism

Because of the view of predication and of signifying that I developed earlier, there is no reason to consider the resemblance theory as any more than a corollary to nominalism. So as the major rivals to realism, we need to investigate only nominalism and the theory of abstract particulars.

A version of nominalism is represented by this passage from Hobbes:

> Of names, some are *proper,* and singular to one only thing, as *Peter, John, this man, this tree;* and some are *common* to many things, *man, horse, tree*; every of which, though but one name, is nevertheless the name of divers particular things; in respect of all which together, it is called an *universal*; there being nothing in the world universal but names; for the things named are every one of them individual and singular.[1]

This is the common name theory of predication. On this view the predicate-word in

(1) This leaf is green

is to be interpreted as a name, not the name of a quality to be sure, but the name of each of those things that has the quality.

There are two ways of interpreting this theory, both of which lead to absurdities. Let us think of (1) as being spoken

1. Thomas Hobbes, *Leviathan,* chap. 4.

by some person at a particular time to make a true statement about a particular leaf. According to the first interpretation, the word "green" as it occurs in this utterance
functions as a name of each and every green thing in the
universe. But then what can be said by the use of (1)? That
this leaf is every green thing in the universe? Certainly this
is incompatible with what (1) really says.[2] According to
the second interpretation, the person who utters (1) is
using "green" as a name of only one green thing, namely,
the thing named by "this leaf." And what he says is true
if and only if the thing named by "this leaf" is identical
with the thing named by "green." But this interpretation
has difficulties of its own. Suppose the speaker of (1) is
subject to an illusion, the leaf really being brown; then (1)
turns out to be false. However, it could be false only if
"green" named something different. But the speaker could
hardly be mistaken about the object he was naming, since
that is before him; his is an error concerning its quality.
So the theory cannot account for certain simple forms of
error.

How, then, can nominalism interpret predication? An approach that avoids the absurdities of the common name
theory is suggested in this passage by Quine.

> One may admit that there are red houses, roses, and sun-
> sets, but deny, except as a popular and misleading man-
> ner of speaking, that they have anything in common. The
> words "houses," "roses," and "sunsets" are true of sundry

2. The common name theory must not be confused with the view
that "green" is the name of the class of all green things and that (1)
asserts that this leaf is a member of the class. For the theory says
that "green" is the name of each green thing taken distributively, not
collectively. Moreover, the class view is subject to the same criticism
as the view that predicates are names of qualities.

individual entities which are houses and roses and sunsets, and the word "red" or "red object" is true of each of sundry individual entities which are red houses, red roses, red sunsets; but there is not, in addition, any entity whatever, individual or otherwise, which is named by the word "redness," nor, for that matter, by the word "househood," "rosehood," "sunsethood." That houses and roses and sunsets are all of them red may be taken as ultimate and irreducible.[3]

Like the classical nominalists, Quine denies that the word "red" names a color quality that different red objects have in common. According to him, the word is not a name at all, either singular or common; its function in the sentence "O is red" is explained by saying that if O is red, then "red" is true of O. However, unlike the classical nominalists, Quine does not claim that the fact that "red" is true of various objects explains how it is that each of them is red. In this passage he suggests that there is no explanation; that various objects are red, he says, is "ultimate and irreducible."

On this account when "O is red" is true, then "O" names O, and "red" is true of O. Both naming and being true of are linguistic functions that have in common the fact that a word which names an object and one which is true of it both apply to that object. What, then, is the difference between naming and being true of if both are cases of applying to an object? Upon initial reflection, the correct answer would seem to be one that offers a quantitative criterion, namely, that "O" applies to just one object and "red" to many. This criterion conforms to a traditional way of understanding the difference between singular and general words.

3. Quine, *Logical Point of View*, p. 10.

However, in another context, Quine points out that the quantitative difference is not always there.

> But actually the difference between being true of many objects and being true of just one is not what matters to the distinction between general and singular. . . . For "Pegasus" counts as a singular term though true of nothing, and "natural satellite of the earth" counts as a general term though true of just one object.[4]

The difference now is to be explained in terms of contrasting grammatical roles.

> It is by grammatical role that general and singular terms are properly to be distinguished. The basic combination in which general and singular terms find their contrasting roles is that of *predication*. . . . Predication joins a general term and a singular term to form a sentence that is true or false according as the general term is true or false of the object, if any, to which the singular term refers.[5]

Predication is introduced to explain the contrast between general and singular because the quantitative criterion used to distinguish naming from being true of was inadequate. Yet in this passage, predication is itself described in terms of the distinction between naming and being true or false of something. We have here an explanatory circle.[6]

4. Quine, *Word and Object*, p. 95.
5. Ibid., p. 96.
6. Quine adds: "General and singular terms, abstract or concrete, are not to be known only by their role in predication. There is also the use of singular terms as antecedents of 'it,' and the use of general terms after articles and under pluralization. Predication is but part of a pattern of interlocking uses wherein the status of a word as general or singular term consists." Ibid., p. 119. But "red" can serve as

Of course one can formulate grammatical criteria to distinguish singular from general terms. Merely in passing I
shall sketch an approach to such a criterion for singular
terms. First, we have to specify what words we wish to
comprehend in the class of singular terms; the usual list
includes proper nouns such as "Socrates" and "Paris"; abstract singular terms such as "equality" and "triangularity,"
and definite descriptions such as "the father of Plato."[7]
Next we specify a set of sentence frames, for example,

———is red
———is an animal

and stipulate that an expression which fits into the empty
space in any of the frames is to count as a singular term
in English. By "fitting into" I mean, not that the entire
sentence must turn out to be true or even to have a truth-
value,[8] but merely that it must be grammatical.[9] This stip-
ulation is too broad, since it includes items that we may
not wish to count as singular. For any such items it is necessary to place restrictions upon the criterion. Let me give two
examples. First, "nothing" fits into "———is red" but per-

an antecedent of "it" as in "Did you see the red color of the table?"
"Yet, it is striking." Also "red" resists articles and pluralization. Quine
has now appeared to give up trying to explain the distinction. See his
"Reply to Stawson," in *Synthese* 18 (December 1968): 293-94.

7. Other candidates often included are pronouns, indefinite descriptions such as "a brother of Plato," number expressions such as "5,"
clauses such as "whoever stole the money." By the approach that
follows, the criterion could be broadened or narrowed to include or
exclude these as required.

8. For example, there are doubts whether "Equality is red" has a
truth-value.

9. If "Equality is red" is to count as grammatical, then we are here
abstracting from our knowledge of which semantic categories go with
which.

haps should not be counted as a singular term.[10] Now "Nothing is red" entails "There are no red things," whereas none
of our standard examples entails this. We can thus qualify
the criterion to exclude terms that yield such an entailment.
Second, "the whale" fits into "——is an animal" even though
the resulting sentence does not say of any particular whale
nor of the class of whales that it is an animal. Rather "The
whale is an animal" is equivalent to "All whales are animals."
Thus we again restrict the criterion to exclude those terms
that yield the equivalence between "The A is an animal" and
"All A's are animals."

This approach, which involves setting up a grammatical
criterion and then restricting its application in various ad hoc
ways, is perfectly consistent with nominalism as it is with
realism. But I have already raised a doubt as to whether the
problem of universals is susceptible of solution by means of
linguistic considerations alone. That "red" signifies the color
red does not establish the existence of the color, nor does it
have any bearing on the question whether quality is an ultimate category, nor does it establish any identity criterion
for qualities. Similarly, linguistic criteria for distinguishing
singular from general terms and subjects from predicates
will turn out to be ontologically neutral. How, then, can we
come to grips with nominalism? There are two ways: first,
by showing that the reasons that lead people to nominalism
are unjustified; second, by establishing that there is a fundamental fact of our experience that nominalism fails to account for.

One argument for nominalism is the objection to multiple
location. If realism is true, there can be entities located at

10. If we wish to exclude "nothing," then perhaps we want our list
of singular terms to coincide with the list of those terms that can be
used to single out or identify possible subjects of discourse.

different places at the same time, and this is thought to be
unintelligible. But there are other versions of particularism,
such as the theory of abstract particulars, which admit
qualities but also deny multiple location. So nominalism
is not necessary to preserve single location.

A second argument is based upon the fact that realism
tends to be associated with rationalism in the history of
philosophy.[11] This is probably based upon the fact that in
some versions of realism universals have no spatiotemporal
location at all, and thus a priori forms of cognition are
posited as the basis for our knowledge of them.[12] Empiricists tended also to assume that whatever does have spatiotemporal location, and hence is perceptible, is a particular.
So empiricists tended to be nominalists. But this assumption,
common to both classical rationalism and classical empiricism, is unjustified. Quine himself has suggested that the
fact that something is observable does not settle the question as to what category it belongs.[13] That one can see
qualities such as colors and shapes leaves open the question
of their classification. So there is no need for empiricists to
lean toward nominalism.

Upon reflecting on certain elementary forms of experience,
we can identify things we know about experience that do
not seem accountable in nominalisitic terms. Consider a
simple experience such as a visual perception of a green,
square patch of color. We know, first, that the patch has at
least two qualities—a color green and a shape square. Second,
we know that the qualities are different from each other.
And third, we know that the color green is an entity quite

11. For example, see the passage by Alonzo Church quoted on
p. 11.
12. See, for example, Bertrand Russell, *Problems of Philosophy*
(London: Oxford University Press, 1912), chaps. 9 and 10.
13. Quine, *Word and Object*, p. 236.

different in nature from the word "green" and that the
shape square is an entity quite different in nature from the
word "square." Fourth, we know upon reflection that the
existence of a green spot does not depend upon the existence of the word "green," nor, for that matter, upon any
other word, and that the existence of a square spot does
not depend upon the existence of the word "square" nor
any other word. We know this in the same way that we
know that the existence of dinosaurs did not depend upon
the existence of human beings, that is, we have secure evidence, in both cases, that the one existed before the other.

The first two things we know imply that the patch is something complex. To say, however, that the patch's being green
and being square are "ultimate and irreducible" is in effect
to deny what we in fact know, that the patch is complex.
And its complexity is susceptible of explanation, namely,
by saying that it has at least two constituents, that signified by "green" and that signified by "square." The second
pair of things we know excludes the nominalist's reply that
the complexity is to be explained, not by reference to qualities that are among the constituents, but by reference to
the multiplicity of words that are true of the patch. For we
know that there is no dependence, de facto or logical, between the patch's being green or square and the applicability
of certain words to it. Neither natural recurrence nor qualitative complexity is a linguistic fact. And that is sufficient
to dispense with nominalism.

Realism versus the Theory of Abstract Particulars

"A character characterizing a concrete thing or individual
is as particular as the thing or individual which it characterizes."[14] This is G. F. Stout's brief summary of the doctrine

14. G. F. Stout, "Universals and Propositions," p. 386.

of particularized qualities, with which he is so closely identified. In replying to G. E. Moore's criticism of the doctrine,
he formulated his view as the assertion that "characters are
abstract particulars which are predicable of concrete particulars."[15] Qualities are the paradigm examples of abstract
particulars. Consider two round dark green patches of the
same size lying side by side on a white background; call one
"Left" and the other "Right." To say of each that it is
round and dark green is to predicate a shape and a color of
each or to characterize each by mentioning a shape and a
color. To say that the shape and color predicated are particulars means that, though they are qualitatively indistinguishable, nevertheless, the color and shape of Left are not numerically identical with the color and shape of Right. To say that
the color and shape of Left and those of Right are as particular as Left and Right themselves means at least that just as
Left and Right cannot be in two places at once, neither can
their colors nor their shapes. The qualities as well as the
patches are localized in space and time.

New philosophical approaches bring changes not necessarily in theory but in the sort of data believed relevant in
defending and criticizing theories. In our time, data based
on "ordinary language" carry a great deal of weight. It has
been argued that the category of abstract particulars is entrenched in ordinary language. This claim can be clarified
by reference to the grammatical phenomon of the nominalization of the predicate in English. Consider any ordinary
subject-predicate sentence where the subject is a singular
term and the predicate is either a verb phrase or the copula
followed by an adjective or by a common noun preceded

15. G. F. Stout, "Are the Characteristics of Particular Things Universal or Particular?" *Aristotelian Society Proceedings,* Supplementary
Volume (1923), p. 114. This volume also contains G. E. Moore's
criticism of Stout's view.

by the indefinite article. English possesses the resources for constructing out of the constituents of the predicate a word or phrase that is, grammatically, a singular noun phrase. List (1) following gives full subject-predicate sentences, and list (2) provides various nominalizations.

   (1) Socrates is wise.
       The book is red.
       The billiard ball is round.
       Socrates sneezed.
       Socrates walked.
       The dynamite exploded.

   (2) wisdom, being wise
       red, redness, being red
       roundness, being round
       sneezing, a sneeze
       walking, a walk
       exploding, an explosion

In (2) the nominalizations use the materials in the predicate in various ways but do not employ the subject-term. The predicate may be nominalized in another way, in which a definite description is formed using the subject-term as well. This is shown in list (3).

   (3) the wisdom of Socrates
       the red color of the book
       the round shape of the billiard ball
       the sneeze of Socrates
       the walk of Socrates
       the explosion of the dynamite

If one's assumptions about language make one inclined to say that the words and phrases in (2) name or designate or introduce universals, which the sentences in (1) predicate

of the things named by the subject-terms, then, by an osten-
sible parity of reasoning, one may be inclined to assert further
that the phrases in (3) name or designate or introduce particularized qualities and events, which the sentences in (1) also
predicate of the things named by the subject-terms.

That we can form phrases of the type listed in (3) and that
we use them in our conversation and writing have been made
the basis for an argument supporting the category of abstract
particulars. P. F. Strawson formulates the argument thus:

> But we do say such things as "His anger cooled rapidly,"
> "His cold is more severe than hers," even "The wisdom
> of Socrates is preserved for us by Plato." Some philoso-
> phers no doubt made too much of the category of par-
> ticularized qualities. But we need not therefore deny
> that we acknowledge them."[16]

There are two deficiencies in this argument. The first is
that it presupposes an extraordinarily permissive criterion
of ontological commitment. The criterion seems to be that
if a person makes a statement using a sentence with a singular term as subject, then he is committed to the existence
of an entity named by that term and to the ontological
category of which that entity is a member. Thus someone
who uses "The wisdom of Socrates is preserved for us by
Plato" to make a statement is thereby committed to the
category of particularized qualities. But, on the contrary,
one who rejects this category would reply that the sentence
is merely a loose way of speaking and that the same statement could be made by means of a paraphrase, such as
"Plato copied many of the wise sayings uttered by Socrates,"
which does not presuppose the existence of this category.

16. P. F. Strawson, *Individuals, an Essay in Descriptive Metaphysics*
(London: Methuen, 1959), p. 169n.

This response invokes a more stringent criterion: a person is committed to the existence of those entities and categories that he refers to by a singular term (or variable) in the context of discourse about ontology. What he says in informal discourse in unguarded moments does not count for purposes of ontology. It is not the vocabulary actually used, but the one the metaphysician finds himself required to use to state what he thinks is true, that determines the range of his commitments. Consequently, inferences about the ontology of a given speaker based on his everyday use of a certain class of expressions are invalid; the speaker is free to reject the inference. The fact that one can form nominalizations such as those in lists (2) and (3) and that it is convenient to use them in everyday discourse does not imply that speakers of English are thereby committed either to universals or to abstract particulars.

The second deficiency is that even if we should adopt the permissive criterion, this would still not require us to accept abstract particulars. The reason is that the evidence that the items in (3), assuming that they name anything, name abstract particulars is far from conclusive. The data drawn from what we say in casual discourse are indecisive. We could say either, "Descartes has the wisdom of Socrates," or instead, "The wisdom of Socrates is exactly like the wisdom of Descartes." In the first version what we are naming is not a particular that only Socrates possesses but a universal that both Socrates and Descartes have in common.

Let us now consider what the logical form of simple subject-predicate statements comes to according to the doctrine of abstract particulars. Take the sentences "Left is round" and "Right is round." Each contains the same predicate with the same meaning; each is used to ascribe the same thing to both Left and Right. And yet each is supposed to characterize Left and Right with numerically distinct particularized qualities. An adequate characterization of their logical form must be consistent both with what is the same and with what is different in the predications. From hints that Stout provided we can construct the following analysis. Suppose that the roundness of each concrete particular that is round is different from the roundness of every other round concrete particular. Call the class of all such roundnesses Roundness. Every member of Roundness is an instance of it; being an instance of something is that species of the class membership relation that holds between a particularized quality and the class of all qualities exactly similar to it. According to Stout the particularized qualities of a thing characterize it. Let "is characterized by" signify the relation that holds between any concrete particular and its particularized qualities. We can now represent "Left is round" by

(1) There is a quality x such that x is an instance of Roundness and Left is characterized by x.

Although this is not an incorrect representation, it is incomplete, for it fails to bring out the fact that the quality that characterizes Left is particularized and is not a universal. Let us expand (1) into

(2) There is a quality x such that x is an instance of Roundness and Left is characterized by x and no object different from Left is characterized by x.

Since Left is different from Right, it follows that the roundness that characterizes Left is other than the one that characterizes Right. The representation of "Right is round" is exactly the same as (2) with "Right" substituted for "Left." Thus (2) takes account of what is the same and what is different in the predications.

There are several criticisms of the claim that (2) represents

the logical form of "Left is round." Let us consider them
one at a time. (a) According to (2), even the simplest subject-
predicate statements in English are of general form because
they contain both an existential and universal quantifier.
But this means that we cannot make a genuine singular
statement, and that, it is alleged, is absurd. However, this
would be absurd only if one assumes that the most elementary
truths there are are ones that ordinary language possesses the
resources to articulate; there is no need whatever for the advocates of the theory to make this assumption. For them
the most elementary truths are of the form "x is characterized by y" where in place of "x" is the name of a concrete
particular and in place of "y" is the name of a particularized
quality which characterizes only that particular. We have already seen that there is reason to doubt that ordinary language possesses the resources in the form of standard methods
of nominalization to form names of particularized qualities.
The absence of such names would mean only that we have
no need outside of philosophical analysis to express truths
of the most elementary sort. And within philosophical analysis we are interested only in the forms of such truths and
do not need any actual names.

(b) There is a familiar type of criticism based upon the
supposition that the doctrine of abstract particulars implies
an infinite regress. We have assumed that someone who uses
"Left is round" to make a statement is predicating something of Left. By a familiar extension of the notion of a
predicate and of predication we could say that (2) also predicates something of Left. Let "is an A" express what is thus
predicated; (2) can be abbreviated as "Left is an A." The
property that "is an A" signifies is the property of being
uniquely characterized by a particular instance of Roundness. According to Stout's view, whatever is predicable of
something is a character, and all characters are particulars.

So "Left is an A" turns out, upon analysis, to assert that Left is characterized by a particular instance of the property of being characterized by a particular instance of Roundness. By similar reasoning we easily generate a series of such predications with no last member.

A similar regress can be generated in another way. Stout writes, "The subject-predicate relation, though it may be of absolutely the same kind is not numerically identical for diverse subjects."[17] So in "Left is round" not only is Left asserted to be characterized by a particular instance of Roundness, but both Left and that instance are joined by a particular instance of the relation of being characterized by something or other. But then they are both characterized by a particular instance of being characterized by a particular instance of being characterized . . . ad infinitum.

Both regresses are concerned with the characterizing tie. The most common example of this regress has nothing to do with the doctrine of abstract particulars. It simply points out that from "Left is characterized by the property of being round" we can go to "Left is characterized by being characterized by the property of being round," ad infinitum. Strawson has suggested that this regress shows that there is no such thing as the characterizing tie.[18] Alan Donagan has claimed that the regress is vicious, and that it shows that a characterizing tie is impossible.[19] This is a familiar view, but it is unsupportable. First of all, one who advocates a characterizing tie can point out that these regresses are based on the linguistic fact that the phrase "is characterized by" happens to be indefinitely reiterable. But there are other in-

---

17. Stout, "Characteristics of Particular Things," p. 119.
18. Strawson, *Individuals*, pp. 175-76.
19. Alan Donagan, "Universals and Metaphysical Realism," *Monist* 47 (1963): 225-26.

definitely reiterable phrases in English that do not generate
an analogous skepticism. Examples are "it is true that" and
"it happens that." In these cases, one thing we can say with
some plausibility is that the reiterations add no further content to the statements made with them, that they are a purely verbal matter. For example, to say that a statement is
true and to say that it is true that it is true are two ways of
saying the same thing. Similarly, to say that Left is round
and Left is characterized by being round, and so on, is
simply to repeat oneself. There is no problem here; just
an interesting grammatical fact. The existence or nonexis-
tence of a characterizing tie must be argued on other grounds.
Verbal redundancy, even when it can be generated according to rule, does not invariably possess philosophical significance.

In addition to this general response to the charge of an
infinite regress, an advocate of the doctrine of abstract
particulars can add something further. He can and ought
to be cautious and claim that the analysis of the kind illustrated by (2) is intended to apply only to a limited class of
sentences, say, those ascribing a perceptible quality to a
perceptible particular. These sentences represent the range
of the analysis; it need not be applied to any further class
of sentences such as those generated by the analysis presented in (2). Thus the cases where reiteration arises never
occur; there is no reason to use such sentences to make any
statements. One virtue of this cautious approach is that the
concept of a quality or character is restricted in application
and becomes philosophically manageable. Other classes
of characters can be introduced piecemeal as needed. There
is no reason to assert as Stout did that every predicate in
English names a character. The cautious approach means
that one's ontology is not at the mercy of English grammar
and vocabulary.

(c) It seems possible that what (2) asserts to characterize Left is really a universal. Suppose that x and y are different instances of Roundness if they possess diameters of different length. Consider a universe in which no two round objects have the same diameter. In such a universe (2) would be true, even though there is no mention of particularized qualities and even though our description of the universe leaves it an open possibility that different objects are characterized by the same instance of Roundness. Thus (2) does not in itself adequately characterize the doctrine of abstract particulars. One way of restricting the interpretation of (2) to exclude universals from being the values of the variables is to add a principle making use of the concept of necessity. One formulation of the requisite principle is

(3) It is necessary that if two different concrete particulars are characterized by the qualities x and y, then x is numerically distinct from y.

The theory of abstract particulars can be successfully defended against some of the more obvious criticisms. It does not appear to be internally inconsistent. Moreover it does not violate any well-established empiricist requirements because particularized qualities such as colors and shapes are as observable as anything else. There is, however, an argument against the theory that I consider to be conclusive. In order to develop it, it is necessary to present a few ideas concerning the notion of identity.

The notion of identity I shall be concerned with is numerical rather than generic or qualitative identity. When I speak of x being the same as y, I do not mean that x and y are the same kind of thing or that they have some or all of their qualities in common. I mean that they are the exact same thing, in the way that the Empire State Building was, in 1969, the exact same thing as the tallest building in the

world. The view I shall espouse, which I shall call the conceptual theory of identity, is, roughly, that any claim that
x is identical with or the same as y is an elliptical way of
asserting that x is the same A as y, where "A" represents a
concept or a classification. Thus "$2 + 3 = 5$" is short for
"$2 + 3$ is the same as the number 5." And "Scott was the
same as the author of *Waverly*" is elliptical for "Scott was
the same person as the author of *Waverly*."[20]

My reason for holding this view is that to say that x and
y are the same is equivalent to saying that they are one and
not two, and to assert that they are numerically different is
to say that they are two and not one. Judgments of identity
and difference are elementary forms of enumeration; they
express the results of counting. Frege showed that when we
engage in counting a collection of objects, it is not the objects as such that are counted but objects as classified in a
certain way.[21] No entity can be one thing per se; it is not
even clear what this means; rather an entity is one this or
one that, such as one apple or one table. Not any concept-

20. A view much like the conceptual theory was developed by Peter
Geach in "Identity," *Review of Metaphysics* 21 (September 1967),
pp. 3-12. There he writes: "Identity is relative. When one says 'x is
identical with y,' this, I hold, is an incomplete expression; it is short
for 'x is the same A as y' where 'A' represents some count noun . . ."
(p. 3). However, in certain important respects, my view departs from
Geach's so I am not appropriating this terminology.

21. In *The Foundations of Arithmetic* (Oxford: Blackwell, 1953)
Frege argues as follows: "While looking at one and the same external
phenomenon, I can say with equal truth both 'It is a copse' and 'It is
five trees,' or both 'Here are four companies' and 'Here are 500 men.'
Now what changes from one judgment to the other is neither any
individual object, nor the whole, the agglomeration of them, but
rather my terminology. But that is itself only a sign that one concept
has been substituted for another" (p. 59). One can accept this insight
without thereby agreeing with Frege that "the content of a statement
of number is an assertion about a concept" (ibid.).

word will do in place of "A," only those that signify a principle of division of the entities falling under them. I shall call such principles of division *enumerating concepts*. The test of whether some given concept A is an enumerating concept is whether one can provide an answer to the question "How many A's?" The test is whether A can be used for counting. The conceptual theory of identity may now be formulated as the claim that any statement of the form "x is the same as y" is an abbreviation of "There exists an enumerating concept A such that x and y are the same A."

It is wrong to interpret the conceptual theory as implying that objects can be sometimes the same and sometimes different, depending upon the enumerating concepts being used. One might think that if the concept is "color spot," then Left and Right are distinct, but if it is "shape," then they are the same. This interpretation is, however, incorrect. Left and Right, although they are the same in shape, are not and cannot be the same shapes, simply because they are color spots, not shapes. One cannot make correct judgments of identity using concepts that are false of the objects in question. If x is the same A as y, then for any other applicabel enumerating concept B, x is the same B as y. For example, if x is the same table as y, then x is the same piece of furniture as y.

The conceptual theory is perfectly compatible with the standard logic of identity. It is possible to interpret the theorems of this logic in accordance with this theory. Thus the symmetry theorem—"If x is the same as y, then y is the same as x"—is to be interpreted as "For any enumerating concept A, if x is the same A as y, then y is the same A as x." The reflexivity theorem—"x is the same as x"—says, "For any x and for any enumerating concept A that is true of x, x is the same A as x." In applying the logic of identity to a domain of objects, the range of the variables is usually restricted to clarify the enumerating concepts presupposed. If the domain is restricted to numbers, for example, then the symmetry theorem is interpreted as "If x is the same number as y, then y is the same number as x."

Let us return now to the theory of abstract particulars. Left and Right are exactly alike in color and shape. Suppose we apply some standard test—say comparison with a color chart—to determine whether the color of Left is the same shade as that of Right. The test reveals no difference at all. The colors qua colors are qualitatively indistinguishable. The theory says that qualities that are qualitatively indistinguishable may yet be different provided each qualifies a different particular. To say that the colors are qualitatively indistinguishable means that they are the same shade of color; they are certainly not merely resembling shades, for it is part of our notion of a shade that where no difference is discernible we have the same, not similar, shades. But according to the conceptual theory of identity if x and y are the same shade of color, then they are the same; no matter what other concept is applied, they are the same. There is no room for difference.

Stout would say that although x and y are the same shade, they are different entities. But then what is the enumerating concept in virtue of which they are different? Stout would answer that x and y differ positionally; x occurs at position P_1 and y at P_2, and this is the ground of their difference. Things that are qualitatively identical can differ positionally, so there is room for difference after all. Let us suppose, just to simplify matters, that a color spot consists of the sum of a shade of color and its position. It is true that the sum of x and P_1 is a different color spot from the sum of y and P_2. There is a difference under the enumerating concept "color spot." But this fails to establish that x is different from y; it is compatible with their being identical. x and y are colors, not color spots; the two sums are color spots, not colors, although they contain colors as parts. Therefore, a positional difference, though it does lead to a difference in entity, fails to yield a difference in the required kind of entity.[22]

The argument can be generalized as follows: If x and y are any qualitatively indistinguishable qualities, then any difference between them can come only through the addition of different entities to them. Although such an addition creates distinct sums, it fails to establish the nonidentity of the qualities we started with. The fact that x and y are the same shade of color suffices to establish the numerical identity of x and y. No theory that accepts qualities and denies universals can be true.

22. A possible reply would be to insist that the position of the color is a constituent of the color, so that colors at two positions must be different colors. But this seems to be false; a color and a place are not related as whole to part.

10 The Objectivity of Discourse

Performative Objects

Performative actions issue in *performative objects*. When a person makes a statement or asks a question or gives an order, there is a statement he makes, a question he asks, or an order he gives. Statements, questions, and orders are examples of performative objects. How shall we understand this type of entity? What is the relation of performative objects, first, to the action from which they issue and, second, to the sentence in which they are spoken? There has been a tendency to hypostatize performative objects, especially statements—that is, to suppose that these objects have an existence prior to and independent of the associated performative actions. The result has been the theory of propositions, which has already been scrutinized and rejected. This tendency is rooted in the way we speak about performative actions in ordinary language—to say that someone is making a statement is to use a form of words suggesting a phrase such as "sailing a boat," where the object boat does exist prior to and independently of the action of sailing.

But another approach is available. I shall base it upon a series of distinctions introduced by C. J. Ducasse.[1] Consider the following lists:

1. Ducasse employed these distinctions in his criticism of G. E. Moore's theory of sensation. What follows is taken from his collection of essays *Truth, Knowledge, and Causation* (London: Routledge and Kegan Paul, 1968), pp. 195-98.

(1) striking a stroke   (2) striking a man
    waving a farewell   waving a flag
    jumping a jump   jumping a fence
    dancing a dance
    dancing a waltz

Although the phrases in (1) and (2) are, with respect to the
parts of speech out of which they are composed, grammatically alike, there is an obvious and crucial difference between
them. In the case of (1) Ducasse calls the entity named by
the noun the *connate accusative* of the activity signified by
the verb. Thus a stroke, a farewell, a jump, a dance, and a
waltz are accusatives respectively of the activities of striking, waving, jumping, and dancing. But in (2) what the noun
names he calls the *alien accusative* of the corresponding
activity. Thus a man, a flag, and a fence are alien accusatives
respectively of striking, waving, and jumping. The general
principle behind the distinction is formulated by Ducasse
as follows: "Whatever the nature of the activity, an accusative connate with it . . . exists only in occurrences of the
activity."[2] A dance exists only in the dancing of it, a jump
only in the jumping of it, a stroke only in the striking of it,
a farewell only in the waving of it. To say that a dance
exists is to say that someone is dancing it. Particular dances
are species or forms of the general activity of dancing; the
difference, for example, between the waltz and the rhumba
is a difference between species of the activity of dancing.
Ducasse's principle is evident at least with respect to these
examples.

Any tendency due to our language to hypostatize connate
accusatives can be inhibited by using different parts of speech.
Thus, instead of using "dancing a waltz" one can transform

2. Ibid., p. 198. (Italics omitted.)

the noun into an adverb thus: "dancing waltzily." Although
this is an artificial procedure, it can be explained as a thera-
peutic device directed against certain metaphysical ills, not
as a recommendation for ordinary discourse. This device
suggests that the connate accusative of the activity can be
called an adverb of the activity. Thus I shall call Ducasse's
theory the *adverbial theory* of connate accusatives.

I should like to recommend an adverbial theory of performative objects. For the sake of simplicity note that the
phrases "making a statement," "asking a question," and
"giving an order" can be replaced, although clumsily, by
"stating a statement," "querying a query," and "ordering
an order." My claim is that a statement, a query, and an
order are connate accusatives respectively of the activities
of stating, querying, and ordering. In general, a performative
object is the connate accusative of a performative action.
Therefore, to claim that a certain performative object exists—
say, the statement that the cat is on the mat—is to claim that
a certain performative action was performed—the action of
stating that the cat is on the mat. The argument in favor of
the adverbial theory consists of all the reasons against
hypostatizing performative objects. That there are such
things as performative actions there can be no doubt. But
that there are, independent of such actions, all the species
of performative objects, is problematic. The adverbial theory
is the most plausible way of dispensing with the need to
hypostatize.

One may object to the adverbial theory as follows: When
a person makes a certain statement, one can reflect upon
the statement made independently of the particular action
of making it; one can discover the statement's implications
and presuppositions and investigate whether or not it is true.
The fact that one can thus abstract the statement from the
action means that it cannot be identified with the action.

But this argument from abstraction leads to absurdities. Thus one can consider the waltz independently of any particular dancing of it and compare it to other dances. One can formulate quite abstractly the structure of the waltz, yet it would be absurd to distinguish the existence of the waltz from the existence of dancings of it. The fact that one can distinguish a feature of an action and consider it independently fails to establish that it is other than a feature of the action.

Another argument against the adverbial theory is based upon the fact that we predicate truth and falsehood of statements. True statements are truths, and false statements are falsehoods. Since there are admittedly numerous truths that no one has yet thought of or spoken, this seems to mean that there are unspoken statements. So, it would appear, statements cannot be mere connate accusatives. This argument, however, trades upon an ambiguity in "truth." When we speak of a truth, sometimes we have in mind a true statement, but at other times we have in mind a fact that could be expressed by a true statement. A fact is in the world and independent of performative actions, but some performative actions issue in statements which if true express facts. To say that there are truths which no one has yet spoken means merely that there are facts which no one has yet stated. And this is perfectly compatible with the adverbial theory.

But what about truth itself? The adverbial theory is committed to a view such as the following: Suppose Jones makes the true statement that the cat is on the mat. This means that he stated the true statement that the cat is on the mat where the statement is the connate accusative of the stating. The phrase "that the cat is on the mat" describes the type or form of stating that it is; it describes a feature of the stating that can be abstracted and considered separately. To say that the statement was true means that he stated it truly. Truth itself as a property of statements is a feature of forms of stating. Other things that we say about statements can also be understood as assertions about actual or possible statings. For example, to say that the statements *p* and *q* are logically inconsistent means that no one can, logically, truly state that *p* and *q*. To say that *p* entails *q* is to say that *p* and not *q* are inconsistent. Our discourse about statements is an abbreviated form of discourse about statings.[3]

An alternative account of statements that is widely accepted is to identify a statement with the declarative sentence that is used to make it. A defect of the theory is that the same statement can be made using a variety of different sentences. The adverbial account avoids this problem because it concedes that the same stating may issue from different linguistic materials.

Actions as Universals

Whether different persons use the same or different words in making a statement, how is it possible for them to make the same statement? Since each performs his own action of stating, how do the different actions eventuate in the same statement?

Actions are a species of events, and events are considered by most philosophers to be particulars or individuals. It is common to distinguish between the particular event—sometimes called a token event—and the type of the particular token. For example: "Any token event E, and any token action A, are by definition particulars. . . . It is logically impossible that two

3. A view similar to the adverbial theory developed here is contained in Bruce Aune, "Statements and Propositions," *Nous* 1 (1967): 215-29.

persons should do the same token action."[4] This view could
easily be formulated without using the token-type distinction. Thus:

> The word "act" . . . is used ambiguously in ordinary lan-
> guage. It is sometimes used for what might be called
> act-qualifying properties, e.g. theft. But it is also used
> for the individual cases which fall under these proper-
> ties, e.g. the individual thefts. . . . The individual cases
> that fall under theft, murder, smoking, etc., we shall call
> act-individuals.[5]

This view appears to have the consequence that the actions
of no two individuals can eventuate in the same performative
object; no two persons can make the same statement, ask the
same question, give the same order although they may make
the same type of statement or ask the same type of question
or give the same type of order. We can avoid this unwelcome
result by dismissing the theory from which it stems. Note
that the theory that actions are particulars can be understood
as an application of the theory of abstract particulars. Grammatically, actions appear to have the same status as qualities.
Just as in "The book is green" the predicate "green" signifies
a certain color that the sentence is used to ascribe to the book,
so in "John runs" the verb "runs" signifies a certain action
that the sentence is used to ascribe to John. And the reason
we gave for thinking that the color is a universal applies also
to the action. Just as two different things can have numerical-

4. B. A. O. Williams, "Personal Identity and Individuation," in
Essays in Philosophical Psychology, ed. D. F. Gustafson (New York:
Doubleday, 1964), p. 328.

5. G. von Wright, "Deontic Logic," reprinted in *Contemporary
Reading in Logical Theory,* ed. Irving Copi and James Gould (New
York: Macmillan, 1967), pp. 303–04.

ly the same shade of color, so two different persons can
perform numerically the same action. There is no token-
type distinction to be drawn.[6]

For how could we draw such a distinction? Consider: both
Jones and Smith raise their arms. Perhaps we can find some
differences, for Jones raised his left arm quickly and Smith
his right arm slowly. There are differences in detail, and
this allows us to say that they did different things. Suppose
instead that both raise their left arms quickly. The differences by which we grounded a distinction of action are no
longer there. The advocate of a type-token distinction for
actions will now argue that there still is a difference, one
that is inevitable, which can ground the requisite distinction.
After all, Jones's raising his arm was done by Jones at, say,
10:00 A.M. and Smith's was done by Smith at, say, 11:00 A.M.
The difference in agent and in time yields the result that what
Jones did could not be done by Smith just because Jones is
not Smith and 10:00 A.M. is not 11:00 A.M.

But what, I ask, does this supposed difference amount to?
True, "Smith's raising his arm at 11:00 A.M." and "Jones's
raising his arm at 10:00 A.M." are different phrases—the first
designates what Smith did and the second what Jones did.
But from that it does not follow that they did different
things. The difference in the agent and the time are not differences in what was done. By analogy, suppose Smith owns
a car and so does Jones. The phrase "Smith's car" and "Jones's
car" are different linguistic materials. But if they own the same

6. For a fuller justification see Charles Landesman, "Actions as Universals," *American Philosophical Quarterly* 6 (July 1969): 247-52. An
alternative account is formulated by Donald Davidson, "The Logical
Form of Action Sentences," in the *Logic of Decision and Action*, ed.
Nicholas Rescher (Pittsburgh: University of Pittsburgh Press, 1966),
pp. 81-95. My response to Davidson is in "Abstract Particulars,"
Philosophy and Phenomenological Research (forthcoming).

car jointly, then the different phrases name the same object. There is no more reason to classify actions as particulars than to do so for qualities.

What is wanted is an explanation of the objectivity or interpersonal nature of discourse. The same statement can be made, the same question asked, the same order given by different speakers at various places and times. The linguistic actions of different persons can issue in identical performative objects. Can this be understood without hypostatizing performative objects, without making them into things that exist apart? If different persons can perform numerically the same actions and if performative objects may be construed as the connate accusatives or adverbs of actions, then different persons can produce the same performative objects. The objectivity of discourse is assured. This is a welcome result. It shows that a theory of the type developed here, which explains meaning in terms of certain psychological states of speakers, can avoid the twin perils of Platonic hypostasis and solipsism. Speakers are not required to attach their discourse in a mysterious way to meanings that exist apart, nor are they locked into a private world from which there is no exit. Performative objects are repeatable aspects of a public world.

Index

Abstract particulars: theory of, 127, 128n, 136-38, 140-43, 145, 146, 149-50
Actions: as universals, 155-58. *See also* Linguistic action
Adverbial theory, 151-55
Alston, William, 18n, 26n, 45-46
Ambiguity: and intention of speaker, 1, 61; and sentence-meaning, 5-6; and propositions, 6; and linguistic action, 22
Aristotle, 87n
Aune, Bruce, 155n
Austin, J. L.: on illocutionary force, 22-24; on performatives, 28, 31, 33-35, 39; on conventions, 42-43, 58

Behaviorism, 4, 97
Belief: and statements, 64-66; paradox of, 67-68
Bergmann, Gustav, 85n, 111-12

Carnap, Rudolf: critique of psychologism, 5
Categories, 123, 125-27, 135, 140
Category explanation, 120
Characterizing tie, 144-45
Chisholm, Roderick, 88n
Chomsky, Noam, 15, 51n
Church, Alonzo, 11-12
Cohen, L. J., 23n, 27n

Conventions: as basis of meaning, 2-3, 83; and natural regularities, 43-44; origination in agreement, 44-45; and rules, 44-45; and purpose, 55-56, 70, 72, 79, 83; arbitrariness of, 56; expectations involved in, 56-57; existence of, 73; and word meaning, 79; and intentional states, 84n

Davidson, Donald, 157n
Definition, 74-79
Dictionaries, 50, 94, 96
Donagan, Alan, 144
Ducasse, C. J., 151-53

Empiricism, 136
Enumerating concepts, 148
Existence claims, 122-23

Fodor, Jerry, 19n, 51-52
Frege, Gottlob: critique of psychologism, 4-5; on counting, 147

Geach, Peter, 147n
General terms, 132-35
Generative-structural attributes, 53
Gestalt psychology, 103, 105
Grice, H. P.: theory of meaning, 62-64, 69, 71, 73, 85

Hart, H. L. A., 51n
Hobbes, Thomas: use of speech,